HOW E[illegible] READINGS MAY CHANGE *YOUR* LIFE

Edgar Cayce, America's most famous clairvoyant, had remarkable, often startling insights into the mysterious world of dreams.

All of this book comes directly from Edgar Cayce's hundreds of dream-interpretation readings, never before studied in their entirety, and therefore is the truly authentic "Cayce on dreams."

Dr. Harmon H. Bro, the only trained social scientist ever to study Edgar Cayce at first hand, interprets the wisdom of Edgar Cayce in a way that makes it practical for every reader.

For millions of Americans fascinated by the extraordinary phenomenon of Edgar Cayce, and for those who wish to gain greater happiness through a deeper understanding of their unconscious dream world, this is *the* essential book.

Books In
The Edgar Cayce Series

THERE WILL YOUR HEART BE ALSO
DREAMS YOUR MAGIC MIRROR
EDGAR CAYCE ON DIET AND HEALTH
EDGAR CAYCE ON HEALING
EDGAR CAYCE ON RELIGION AND
PSYCHIC EXPERIENCE
EDGAR CAYCE ON ESP
THE EDGAR CAYCE READER
EDGAR CAYCE ON ATLANTIS
THE EDGAR CAYCE READER #2
EDGAR CAYCE ON DREAMS
EDGAR CAYCE ON PROPHECY
EDGAR CAYCE ON REINCARNATION
EDGAR CAYCE ON JESUS AND HIS CHURCH
EDGAR CAYCE ON THE DEAD SEA SCROLLS

Published By
WARNER BOOKS

EDGAR CAYCE ON DREAMS

by Harmon Hartzell Bro, Ph.D.

under the editorship of
Hugh Lynn Cayce
Director, Association for
Research and Enlightenment

WARNER BOOKS

A Warner Communications Company

WARNER BOOKS EDITION

Warner Books, Inc.
666 Fifth Avenue
New York, N.Y. 10103

A Warner Communications Company

Printed in the United States of America

First Warner Books Printing: October, 1968

25 24 23 22

TABLE OF CONTENTS

INTRODUCTION

WHO WAS EDGAR CAYCE?

The nine books which have been written about Edgar Cayce have totaled more than a million in sales. Many other books have devoted sections to his life and talents. He has been featured in dozens of magazines and hundreds of newspaper articles dating from 1900 to the present. What was so unique about him?

It depends on through whose eyes you look at him. A goodly number of his contemporaries knew the "waking" Edgar Cayce as a gifted professional photographer. Another group (predominantly children) admired him as a warm and friendly Sunday School teacher. His own family knew him as a wonderful husband and father.

The "sleeping" Edgar Cayce was an entirely different figure—a psychic known to thousands of people, in all walks of life, who had cause to be grateful for his help. Indeed, many of them believed that he alone had either "saved" or "changed" their lives when all seemed lost. The "sleeping" Edgar Cayce was a medical diagnostician, a prophet, and a devoted proponent of Bible lore.

In June, 1954, the University of Chicago held him in sufficient respect to accept a Ph.D. thesis based on a study of his life and work. In this thesis the writer referred to him as a "religious seer." In that same year, the children's comic book *House of Mystery* bestowed on him the impressive title of "America's Most Mysterious Man!"

Even as a child, on a farm near Hopkinsville, Kentucky, where he was born on March 18, 1877, Edgar Cayce displayed powers of perception which seemed to extend beyond the normal range of the five senses. At the age of six or seven he told his parents that he was able to see and talk to "visions," sometimes of relatives who had recently died. His parents attributed this to the overactive imagination of a lonely child who had been influenced by the dramatic language of the revival meetings which were popular in that section of the country. Later, by sleeping with his head on his schoolbooks, he developed some form of photographic memory which helped him advance rapidly in the country school. This gift faded, however, and Edgar was only able to complete his seventh grade before he had to seek his own place in the world.

By the age of twenty-one he had become the salesman for a wholesale stationery company. At this time he developed a gradual paralysis of the throat muscles which threatened the loss of his voice. When doctors were unable to find a physical cause for this condition, hypnosis was tried, but failed to have any permanent effect. As a last resort, Edgar asked a friend to help him re-enter the same kind of hypnotic sleep that had enabled him to memorize his schoolbooks as a child. His friend gave him the necessary suggestion, and once he was in a self-induced trance, Edgar came to grips with his own problem. He recommended medication and manipulative therapy which successfully restored his voice and repaired his system.

A group of physicians from Hopkinsville and Bowling Green, Kentucky, took advantage of his unique talent to diagnose their own patients. They soon discovered that Cayce only needed to be given the name and address of a patient, wherever he was, to be able to tune in telepathically on that individual's mind and body as easily as if they were both in the same room. He needed, and was given, no other information regarding any patient.

One of the young M.D.'s, Dr. Wesley Ketchum, submitted a report on this unorthodox procedure to a clinical research society in Boston. On the ninth of October, 1910, *The New York Times* carried two pages of headlines and pictures. From that day on, troubled people from all over the country sought the "wonder man's" help.

When Edgar Cayce died on January 3, 1945, in Virginia Beach, Virginia, he left well over 14,000 documented stenographic records of the telepathic-clairvoyant statements he had given for more than six thousand different people over a period of forty-three years. These documents are referred to as "readings."

The readings constitute one of the largest and most impressive records of psychic perception ever to emanate from a single individual. Together with their relevent records, correspondence and reports, they have been cross-indexed under thousands of subject headings and placed at the disposal of psychologists, students, writers and investigators who still come, in increasing numbers, to examine them.

A foundation known as the A.R.E. (Association for Research and Enlightenment, Inc., P. O. Box 595, Virginia Beach, Virginia, 23451) was founded in 1932 to preserve these Readings. As an open-membership research society, it continues to index and catalog the information, initiate investigation and experiments, and promote conferences, seminars and lectures. Until now, its published findings have been made available to its members through its own publishing facilities.

This is the fourth volume in a series of popular books dealing with those subjects from the Edgar Cayce readings.

This volume presents the data from more than six hundred Edgar Cayce Readings on dreams.

Harmon H. Bro, Ph.D., worked with Edgar Cayce for the better part of a year—from 1943 to 1944. He observed the regular schedule of daily readings. Coming to Virginia Beach as a skeptic he asked probing questions, interviewed persons who came for readings and read correspondence. Careful detailed notes became the basis for a doctoral thesis a few years later at the University of Chicago.

Recognizing as many students of the Readings have that Edgar Cayce placed unusual emphasis on the value of an individual's study of his own dreams, Dr. Bro has examined and thoroughly indexed the hundreds of dream readings.

Here is his first popular study of these readings. It is designed not only to present the challenging new concepts on dreams which are contained in this psychic's unusual approach to the subject, but also to enable the reader to apply these ideas in working with his own daily dream material.

In my opinion this is one of the best and most important studies ever made of the Edgar Cayce Readings.

—Hugh Lynn Cayce

PART I. THE DREAMS OF A YOUNG WOMAN

CHAPTER I. THE DREAMER

She was young, just twenty-one. She was attractive, proud of her figure. She was ambitious, from a leading Mississippi family. She was bright, a graduate of a select women's college.

And now she was married. She had picked a Pennsylvania banker, eight years older, whom she had met at a family resort. She knew that his associates called his future promising, and she could imagine him on Wall Street someday.

She could hardly guess that within four years he would be not only a Wall Street banker, but a millionaire, a financial marvel even in the prosperous Roaring Twenties.

Right now, freshly married, she had a problem on her hands. How was she to justify to her relatives her husband's consuming interest in a middle-aged Ohio psychic named Edgar Cayce? She had told them about Cayce: her parents, her sister, and most of her uncles, aunts, and cousins. But they had stayed skeptical. She could see why.

Cayce was uneducated. He had no respectable profession at present, although he had been a successful Alabama photographer until a couple of years ago, in 1923, when he had moved to Ohio. He had no money, although not far back he had held a million dollars in oil properties located by his psychic gift for his Cayce Petroleum Company—and had lost it all in drilling gambles and business calamities. He didn't even have a home of his own, for her husband was helping to finance the costs of moving his family to Virginia Beach, Virginia, where Cayce's psychic source had long insisted he would be most productive.

There were only a few things she could say to her relatives in Cayce's favor.

He was a southerner, from good Kentucky stock that

could trace its ancestry back to France, as could some of her own relatives in the Deep South. He was a family man, with a petite but regal southern wife, and one son in third grade and another in high school. He taught Sunday School in the Christian Church, a Baptist-like church which was popular in the South. And he was helping her husband, Aaron, become a rich man.

She had heard story upon story from Aaron, telling how Cayce was coaching him and some Ohio businessmen to use their natural psychic talents to become wealthy. Cayce offered them no miracles, for he gave business counsel only to those who were already active and effective in their fields: manufacturers, real estate brokers, corporation executives, product inventors, distributors, stockbrokers, insurance salesmen and bankers like her husband. Even to these his counsel was limited, she knew. For while he could evidently see an astonishing array of facts with his psychic vision, he called on his talent only to train others to use their own talents: their hunches, their impressions, their promptings, and their dreams. But he had convinced her husband that was all the aid he needed, for he was rapidly becoming wealthy, as were a number of his associates—especially two brothers who were stockbrokers.

Cayce was certain, Aaron had explained to her, that psychic ability was a normal potential in every healthy, creative person. He saw it as an outreach of the personality that could be trained as one might train musical or philosophic or executive abilities.

Frances was especially fascinated with what Cayce could do with dreams. She knew that for months her young husband had been presenting his dreams to Cayce for interpretation—especially on business matters but also on sex, aggression, health, personality patterns, fears, religion, attitudes towards associates, hobbies, death, and even on what sorts of brides his girl friends might become. Now he was encouraging her to present her dreams to Cayce.

So Frances, a bride of one week, wrote down some recent dreams and mailed them to Edgar Cayce in his new home at Virginia Beach, to be interpreted in the trance "readings" which he took twice daily.

She began one of the most colorful chapters in the history of twentieth-century dream interpretation—a century that had started with Freud's monumental volume, *The Intrepretation of Dreams,* but which left dream study in the hands of analysts until its midpoint, when the first "sleep laboratories" began to appear on university campuses.

Frances' dreams, interpreted by Edgar Cayce, may one day prove to be only a novelty in the century which rediscovered dreams. Or they may prove fresh leads to the workings of dreams, to the makeup of dreamers, and to things worth dreaming about.

Over a four-year period she submitted to Cayce, largely by mail, 154 dreams, with which he dealt at varying length in fifty-five of his readings—almost all of them given in the first three years. Only three other persons, one of whom was Cayce himself, submitted such extensive collections of dreams for his psychic analysis. During the two decades after 1924 during which he interpreted dreams, others also sought dream guidance—a total of sixty-nine people before Cayce's death in 1945. All together, Cayce was given some 1650 dreams for his interpretation in about seven hundred readings—approximately one reading in twenty of the thousands that were recorded and saved in the forty years of his psychic efforts.

What sort of dreamer was Frances? What sort of waking life lay behind her dreams?

During the time that Cayce served as her dream analyst, and as her coach in learning to interpret her own dreams, Frances went through both calm times and rough. Her dreams mirrored both.

She lived well in an expensive home in New York City, with servants to do her wishes. She traveled to Europe, and often to her girlhood home in Mississippi, as well as to Virginia Beach, Palm Springs, Florida, and Chicago. She bought lovely clothes. She read a great deal, but she also worked energetically at entertaining. She found time to indulge in lazy memories of her childhood, and in fantasies of old love affairs.

She went through ecstasy when Cayce assured her she would bear a child who could be an intellectual and spiritual leader in her times. Then she had a miscarriage, of which both Cayce and her dreams warned her—and she left the hospital just in time to attend her mother's funeral.

She bore her son at last, over a year later, but before she left the hospital with him, her father died suddenly in Mississippi. Frances knew pain as well as she knew joy, during the time she worked on her dreams with Cayce.

The dream records show that she quarreled with her mother-in-law, but not too bitterly, and always made up. She had her rows with Aaron, too. She was apparently jealous of his intellectual and psychic abilities, while he was inclined to be condescending toward her. But they seemed genuinely fond of each other, and their marriage went along quite well sexually and socially, until it was hit by a series of earthquake-like shocks, all of which were foreshadowed in her dreams.

Eight years after she married Aaron, she divorced him.

Frances does not seem to have been neurotic, although her dreams showed that she could be temperamental, sharp-tongued, stubborn, and even selfish. In most of her dreams she appeared as a fairly normal young woman, going through the adjustments and awakenings of early marriage and motherhood. But she also went through several shocks, which laid bare her personality structure in her dreams.

First, she went through the problem of transference, so familiar to psychoanalysts. She came to see Cayce not only as a father-figure but almost as a prophet, despite his repeated insistence that she turn to the divine, rather than to him, for her devotions. Identifying with Cayce, she showed the familiar love-hate ambivalence: she hoped one day to give readings as he did; she sulked when he did not magically prevent her from her miscarriage. Her resolution of the transference came hard, as it sometimes does in analysis, for she went through a disappointed and nearly permanent rupture with Cayce when her husband (caught in a transference problem of his own) quarreled with Cayce over financing of the Cayce hospital, during Depression days, and withdrew all his support and contact.

Second, Frances experienced the collapse of her security, toward the end of her dream series, when her marriage began to break up.

Third, she underwent a slow but drastic change of religious orientation. She was Jewish, as was her husband, of a fairly liberal though family-oriented tradition which called a house of worship a "temple" instead of a synagogue or "schul." She was familiar with Yiddish phrases and mannerisms, and they helped her defend her dignity as part of a vulnerable minority in American society. She and her relatives went to Jewish resorts, and enjoyed them, as her dreams show.

But it wrenched her that she found Edgar Cayce in his trance state, however tolerant in waking life, adamant that Jesus had in truth been the most complete pattern for men to follow, whatever their religious affiliation. She knew that Cayce did not push her to become a churchgoer, and in fact encouraged her in her hopes of rearing her son to be a religious leader in Israel. But the force of the respect which he gave to the figure of Christ put her under inward stress, as well as under outward tension with relatives.

Fourth, Frances developed what seemed to be a measure of psychic ability of her own. She did not turn towards business affairs, as did her husband, although she developed her ability, as he did, in her dreams. She turned to the woman's world of family and relationships, securing impressions of the health, attitudes, welfare, and potentials of her son, her husband, and her relatives. However great her husband's interest in psychic matters—and he was even more interested in these than in making money, at which he worked hard—she found she could not live in his atmosphere alone. She had to deal with friends and relatives, bustling in and out of her life, and often ridiculing her psychic interests and stories. Her otherwise normal ego was thus put under an unusual strain, and her dreams showed her floundering over how to think of herself and her psychic interests, in front of her peers, despite her wealth and social position.

Frances took four full-strength jolts, besides the death of both parents, in eight years of marriage. It is not surprising that her dreams showed not only the usual stresses, but one major thrust which must have greatly compensated for the blows in her waking life. She began to have vivid dream experiences of her dead mother, whom she came to feel, with Cayce's assurance, was alive beyond the grave. She found in these experiences a source of awe and wonder, as well as practical guidance, which meant a great deal to her—as we shall see.

She never remarried. Later in life she underwent an emotional breakdown, as her dreams with Cayce previewed. She pulled out of it by devotedly serving her son, and by a hard-won career in nursing. The sturdiness which showed in her early dreams seemed to ripen in later years into a strength and compassion which could well have made her a woman to know and to cherish.

CHAPTER II. LEVELS OF DREAMING

As Edgar Cayce interpreted dreams in hundreds of trance sessions, and as he talked about the function of sleep and dreaming in a few essay-type readings, he set forth his view of how dreams work.

They work, he said, to accomplish two things. They work to solve the problems of the dreamer's conscious, waking life. And they work to quicken in the dreamer new potentials which are his to claim.

Why Dreams?

In describing dreams as problem-solving, first of all, Cayce anticipated many of the findings of sleep laboratories which would not be established for another quarter of a century after he counseled Frances.

Although he noted that some of her dreams expressed body-tensions, he did not see her dreams as giving her vicarious satisfaction of subterranean wishes for sex and aggression. Sex and aggression were in her dreams aplenty, and with plots that gratified them. But such dreams, he said, contained more as well; they contained suggestions for how to evaluate and direct these basic drives. Her dreams, he pointed out, would deal with primitive drives only when these became a problem to her; then they would be taken up in dreams as would any other problem, with possible solutions—both realistic and unrealistic—dramatized and evaluated in the dreams.

Although Cayce did not use the term employed by

modern dream researchers in their laboratory work with normal human subjects, he described the process now called the "perseverative effect." It is the process that appears whenever a person becomes involved in a problem or task; he tends to persevere in it until it is worked through. Modern dream research shows that normal people tend to persevere into the night in the questions that absorbed them in the day—not only in questions of their role and status with others, but in very practical questions of money, of studies, of trips, of food, of skills, and even questions of how to get enough sleep.

In describing a large part of dreaming as problem-solving, Cayce also underscored that kind of dreaming which has long interested artists and inventors: the "incubation" dream. This is the dream which either presents a surprising solution to a problem or design on which the dreamer has been working, or awakens him in a state of mind where the solution he needs springs easily to his thoughts. Here, again, Cayce paralleled the work of modern sleep and dream laboratories, some of which today are not only exploring the mind's capacity for creative incubation in dreams, but even its use of ESP in sleep, as part of its problem-solving work.

But when, on the other hand, Cayce described the rest of meaningful dreaming as quickening the dreamer to his own human potentials, he came nearer to the viewpoint of psychoanalysis, in its various schools.

Over and over he pointed out how dreams signal to the dreamer that it is time for him to carry new responsibilities, or to develop more mature values, or to stretch his thinking. Such dreams, he said, are not simply solving practical problems. They are helping the dreamer grow.

He described whole cycles of dreams as devoted to developing a new quality in a dreamer: patience, balance, manliness, altruism, humor, reflectiveness, piety. Some of these self-remaking dreams he saw as coming from the efforts of the dreamer's personality to right itself in breakdown—as psychoanalysts see every day in the dreams of those on their couches. Other such dreams Cayce saw as spontaneous, healthy presentations, occurring when it was time for a new episode of growth in the dreamer's life.

Frances accumulated vivid evidence, in four years of

Cayce's help, that her dreams functioned both to solve her outward problems and to quicken her to inner potentials.

There were plenty of practical problems reflected in her dreams. Many were about arguments with relatives or husband. Some were about travel plans. One was about a cold her husband had caught. Two dealt with a maid who had stolen some clothing from her. Numbers of them dealt with her diet and exercise as she prepared for motherhood. Not a few of them displayed her mannerisms and life style exactly as others would see them. There were even dreams that urged her not to rely too heavily on Cayce, as he pointed out in interpreting them.

But mixed in with these problem-solving dreams, and sometimes part of the same dreams, were dream materials that served a different purpose: arousing Frances to a richer and more mature self. Her dreams appeared to invite her to use her good mind more systematically in study. Others prompted her to give herself more freely to her baby, rather than leave him so much to his nurse. A few dreams confronted her with memorable religious experiences. As Cayce saw her dreams, nearly half of them contained some reference or challenge to her life-orientation, to her ultimate values and commitments, as these showed up in prosaic daily living.

He would not let her use her dreams as a handy divining kit.

What might seem a message of a forthcoming illness, he said, could instead mirror a sick attitude in the dreamer's present behavior. What might seem guidance to an advantageous stock sale could be the dreamer's "stock-taking" on himself or a friend. An awesome bearded man in a dream could well be the dreamer's stern conscience, rather than the heavenly messenger she might rather believe. He made it clear that dreams cannot be approached simply as messages from a higher realm. It is important, he explained, "to differentiate between the spiritual inception and the conscious conception" which appear in dreams.

Yet Cayce did insist to Frances that dreams often incorporate realms of consciousness that are wider than waking, if not higher. They can, he said, draw easily on whatever ESP the dreamer possesses as a natural talent or a developed art, to show him problem-solving items from the future, the distant, the past, or the private.

And there are those dreams, he added, which can bring into play more easily than much of waking consciousness certain structures of great importance to the dreamer. Frances might in dreams contact her own best or higher self; or she might even reach to something beyond herself which Cayce called "the Creative Forces or God." Cayce treated these dream contents, not congenial to either modern laboratory or couch, with great respect. Though he picked out a small minority of dreams as embodying explicit, direct contact with the higher self, or with the divine, he did not hesitate to identify some dreams in this way—and thus his dream interpretations come under some question in the century which has rediscovered dreams in the laboratory and the clinic, but not in the church.

Often he summarized the function of dreams in words such as those which he used for a businessman, whom he urged to consult his dreams for "self-edification, and for the building up of the mental and spiritual, as well as the financial, self."

As Cayce counseled Frances and others about their dreams, it became clear that he saw their dreams as coming from different levels within them. In this view the dreamer is somewhat analogous to a ship.

The Level of the Body

The ship is a big machine. It has a hull, engines, propeller, decks, steering devices, anchors. Some of its equipment must be operated by the crew. Some of its equipment, such as life jackets, can be used by passengers. Some of its equipment operates to serve other equipment—as do governors, emergency circuits, oiling devices, and automatic pilots.

In dreams, as Cayce saw them, the dreamer's body presents its operating problems just as the machinery of a ship occupies those who sail it. The body's need for exercise, sleep, a balanced diet, play, hard work, healthy eliminations, medical care, sexual orgasms, quiet meditation—all of these and more seemed to him to crowd the stage of dreams, as expressions of what Cayce called "the physical." To be sure, Cayce said, some dreams originating in the body are merely hallucinogenic, and not worth interpreting, produced by the same body chemistry that prompts the visions of an alcoholic, the mirages on the desert, or the fantasies of a man in deep fatigue.

Still other body-originated dreams, in Cayce's view, are products of the body working on itself, as some of a ship's machinery call other machinery into play.

When Frances asked him to recall for her one dream she had forgotten, as he often did, he said that this one was merely the body giving itself a workout, and did not require study or interpretation.

Still other dreams, Cayce explained, show the body calling for aid which its own mechanisms alone can't supply. Frances dreamed:

> *Saw the boat* Leviathan *and cousin Ted and his wife very sick; and it seemed something was the matter with Ted, and he was dead, for his wife was in a mourning veil.*

Cayce pointed out that she had been thinking of taking an ocean trip, and speculating what seasickness might do to her—or might do even more drastically to her cousin Ted, who was ill at the time. This imagining set the body astir (somewhat as hypnotic suggestion can easily do) with fear of seasickness, fear that caused the dream. (Happily, Cayce not only interpreted the dream, but prescribed for Frances a sensible compound medication which he had given to others to prevent seasickness, with surprisingly good results—considering that it came from an unconscious, uneducated psychic.) Frances' body-machinery got the help for which it seemed to have signaled.

The Level of the Subconscious

A ship is operated by a crew. They are trained to make it run day after day, which they often do automatically. Sometimes their orders conflict, and they must iron out their differences in duties and routines. Sometimes they receive cargo or passengers which they are not trained to handle, and they must question the load. Sometimes they are baffled by machinery or storms, and must appeal to higher authority for help. Sometimes they are given new shipmates with skills or equipment they did not know existed.

Cayce referred to the "subconscious" or the "subconscious forces" in dreams much as one might refer to the crew of a ship. These "forces" he saw as very common in dreams, whether presenting problems of their own functioning, or presenting special information which they have retrieved by their own ESP radar. The language of these forces he saw as characteristically "emblematic"—somewhat like the salty dialects and figures of speech of seamen. The dreamer's subconscious—his hidden structures, habits, controls, mechanisms, complexes, formulas—uses the dreamer's own peculiar memory-images and figures of speech to get things done.

Sometimes the crew of the subconscious may, in the Cayce view, give the body-machinery a dry run in dreams, to prepare it for a forthcoming workout.

Frances had been through a miscarriage, and had some earlier fears of childbirth, when her dreams came up with the following vivid experience. The time was a little more than nine months before her baby was actually born. Cayce's dream interpretation included a challenge that she choose now to become pregnant, and a promise of a happy outcome. Her dream, he said, was caused by her subconscious, which he saw as having charge of all vital functions, giving to her "body-conscious that experience of the condition through which the entity passes to attain" childbirth.

Her crew was warming up the machinery of sexual and maternal instinct. Frances reported:

I had some inner trouble that prevented my having a baby. The doctors told me that to have it corrected would necessitate a slight operation. I objected on the grounds that I couldn't take either. "Oh yes you can," they replied, and I found myself on the operating table being given the anesthetic. Slowly I felt myself losing consciousness under this influence. I felt their fingers grow lighter in touch and their voices seem further and further away. I was unconscious of myself losing consciousness, and of the latter's consummation. Then I came to—regained consciousness, the operation having been done. I mentioned to the nurse that I supposed now I could not have a baby. She replied that I could—very soon. I wanted to get up and go out.

In interpreting this dream, which he saw as wholly positive and encouraging, Cayce not only touched on the theme of motherhood, but picked up, as any analyst would, the word "consummation" which Frances had used to describe her "operation." He suggested to her that the word referred not simply to childbirth as the consummation of her preparation for motherhood, but to sexual release, which she could choose as pleasantly and safely as the dream showed in the touch of fingers and the drifting off to unconsciousness.

Her crew had set the machinery humming.

Frances' dreams showed her continuous concern with the people she held close. They showed her struggling not only with her personal relationships with them, but with their own problems. What bothered them bothered her, because she carried them in her psyche—as a ship carries passengers.

She knew, for example, that her husband longed for a direct psychic experience of his dead father. In her concern for his longing, she had a unique psychic experience of her own, a cryptic but lovely little dream that proved prophetically accurate: *"Saw five chrysanthemums on the grave of my husband's father."*

Cayce responded that in five weeks her husband would have an experience of being taught in dreams by his dead father, which would bring him some of the greatest joy of his life. Five weeks later, right on schedule, the dreams came to Aaron.

Frances had spoken aloud about the flowers, in her sleep, and Cayce commented on this performance, as well. The same subconscious, he said, which had looked ahead to the contents of her husband's dreams had also prompted her to speak aloud about them, and to interpret the dream. But the sound of her own voice had wakened her as she spoke. She could, he continued, train herself to let the subconscious have more initiative, so that such experiences could become spontaneous little "readings" for those she cared about. Her speaking out loud in sleep would be not unlike his own trances, and quite natural expressions, once in a while, of what went on in her dreams. Frances tried, somewhat gingerly, to encourage her subconscious crew to take over in this way.

The next time she talked out loud in her sleep, it was to advise her husband not to change toothpastes! Modest counsel, but sound, according to Cayce. Later her ventures took her much deeper, though the experiences were infrequent. One of the most important found her talking out loud about her own preoccupation with "looks," with her face and figure—a theme which Cayce said was a central motif in her personality, because of its overtones of power over men.

Not every passenger in Frances' ship was easy to handle, as Cayce pointed out in response to another dream she sent him:

> *All of us, my mother-in-law, her friends, my husband and I were back home in Mississippi, way back in the old days when we lived downtown. We were preparing to go to Sandy Beach for the summer. My mother's friend said she wouldn't go, but was going home to White Plains, New York. Mrs. B., another friend, said she would go back to the beach with us. We all got into automobiles and started. Then my mother-in-law got very angry and irritable with me, as she was this past summer. Was very unpleasant.*

Cayce contended that Frances' subconscious (or what might be called her crew) had picked up on its ESP the response that would be forthcoming from relatives and friends in the near future, to some things Frances was going to say or do. He urged her to be prepared for this unpleasantness, and not to let it upset her unduly.

The Level of Consciousness

In most dreams Cayce saw calls to conscious decision and action. The process was like the crew of a ship appealing to the captain for his orders.

As he started to discuss the motherhood dream already mentioned, Cayce commented that anyone who could dream and remember it was capable of learning from dreams, capable of adding conscious insight and behavior to the unconscious impact of the dream experience: "For as we find," he said, "each and every inidvidual who is possessed of the faculty of visioning the various conditions of experiences which pass through the various consciousness of an individual"—he meant the various levels active in dreams—"is capable also of gaining those lessons or truths from same which are . . . the truth as shown to the individual through the various phases of its consciousness."

Nobody dreams who is unable to interpret and learn from his own dreams.

Every man's crew has a captain who must act like one, when the crew approaches him in dreams.

Sometimes the crew might appeal to the captain against the captain!

In the first few weeks of marriage, when Frances was fairly intoxicated with Cayce's interpreting of her dreams, and with his entire outlook on life, she plunged into psychic and occult studies. Like her impatient husband, she wanted to understand the whole business at once, so that she could begin practicing her own small psychic feats. Then she dreamed:

> *Saw myself going down a large chute into water. It widened as I neared the bottom, and branched out in two directions. Someone said, "It is fourteen feet there where you land. What will you do then?"*

Cayce observed that Frances was being warned from within herself that the "mental forces"—her own captain or consciousness—were pushing her beyond her depth, at a time when she was just beginning to understand "elemental conditions" of psychological development. If she would take the time to move "step by step," he said, her mind would broaden in a healthy way, showing her new avenues for using its energies, as the dream depicted with the broadened chute. But if she forced her development by "will," she would bring "destructive forces" onto herself.

The captain had to chart a wise course.

In Cayce's view the captain of consciousness also has definitive powers in determining the cargo for the crew to handle. He saw the subconscious as highly active, constantly molding and shaping whatever was put in its care. Over and over he insisted that "thoughts are things," that "thoughts are deeds," because of their impact on the subconscious.

Frances moved in social circles where bridge and small talk could occupy many hours of a day, building an undercover pettiness that could not always be seen, until one day a part of the bridge player had become a glowering shrew. This dream showed her as much:

> *Regarding the playing of bridge, I beheld standing in front of me right in the room, as real and living, the Queen of Clubs. I became frightened and jumped for my husband.*

Cayce explained that whatever consciousness dwells on is stored in the subconscious, or "stamped upon the subconscious forces," until it takes on body and form and an independent life of its own.

A new figure had joined Frances' crew in this dream, a Frankenstein's monster created at the bridge table where the captain played and gossiped.

The Level of the Superconscious

A crew needs information from beyond the ship, to operate it effectively. Some of this it can secure by its own devices. In times past, sailors took bearings from the stars, time from the sun, news from passing ships.

Cayce spoke repeatedly of the capacity of the subconscious to get its bearings on practical matters by the use of its own natural ESP. He told Frances that it was her own natural psychic talent that brought her unknowns in many of her dreams, from toothpaste to the future behavior of relatives.

But in Cayce's view another source of help is also available. He called it the superconscious, which he described as a higher realm of the subconscious.

Modern sailors might be turning to something like this if they radioed to home port for guidance from a computerized maritime institute, one which could tell them instantly the latest information on ocean currents, on tides, on weather, on other shipping, on their passengers, and even on the markets in ports ahead of them.

Cayce insisted that there are what he called "Universal Forces" that the individual can contact, according to his need and his training to use them. These forces can provide him with boundless information, and with relevant patterns of guidance. They are in effect the creative currents of the divine itself, moving through human affairs like some great unseen Gulf Stream.

In dreams one may reach far beyond his own faculties to tune in on these Universal Forces, through his own superconscious.

Early in her dream study with Cayce, while still uncertain what to make of Cayce's religious outlook, Frances recorded the following:

> *Dreamed I had an earache and was waiting for my mother in front of a drugstore in my old home town. My mother came and my ear hurt so, I wanted her to take me to a doctor. "You don't need one," she said. "You can overcome that yourself." I did and it so surprised me that I went driving with my friend C., and told her all about it. "What you need," she said, "is Christian Science. You ought to try it, for that is Christian Science. Become a Christian Scientist." "No," I replied, "I have my own science. Jewish Science. I cured myself, just naturally."*

In interpreting the dream, Cayce evinced no surprise at her ear trouble, for Frances had already brought him a warning dream of an old mastoid condition. Nor did he comment at length on the manner of healing in the dream. Such aid from the superconscious was as real to him as aid from the medications which he had already prescribed for her ear. He took up, instead, the question of whether such aid from the superconscious is the private property of any one faith. Her dream, he said, was showing her that such forces and energies are objective realities which may be found and used by anyone who will meet their conditions, including "faith in the God-force manifest in an individual, see?" He urged her to study the laws of such aid in healing, no matter who claimed to have a corner on them, nor how offensive they might seem to her friends and relatives. Man may divide up his theories into traditions, Cayce observed, but man is talking about laws that could not be parceled out, for "they remain a oneness, whether Jewish, Gentile, Greek or heathen."

The crew has a resource of energy and guidance beyond anything on shipboard, if they know how to contact home port for it, and really need it.

The Level of the Soul

A ship is operated by its crew, working under orders from the captain. But the captain in turn is subject to orders which he violates at his peril. He is answerable to the owner of the ship.

In the Cayce view, unlike that of some modern psychology, the picture of the total person is not complete without including the owner, the best self, or the soul. This part of the person, well-removed from consciousness, carries his real ideals and commitments, whether verbally formulated or not. It gives character and flavor to his conscience (a function of the subconscious according to Cayce), but the soul is not limited to the conscience. It is also a structure more enduring than consciousness, that captain of daily life, for the soul survives death, and consciousness does not.

The soul determines how long and well the captain and crew endure in their task. It sets their large course for them, while leaving them the daily operation of the vessel. It may, as owner of the ship, make its own representations to the captain through dreams. But its desires may be frustrated by the captain, for decision and action—and therefore growth—are his on the voyage of a lifetime.

After Frances' baby was born, and she was past the critical strains of birthing, she grew careless about diet, laxatives, physiotherapy, her temper, and other matters which she had concluded in her dream study with Cayce were important to her own health and peace of mind, as well as to the baby's. Then she dreamed the following:

> *It seemed I was to marry cousin William, but when it came to it I hesitated because he was my cousin and he had had so much trouble. Thus I hemmed and hawed and hesitated, undecided what to do.*

Cayce warned her that her now "real inner self," her "self's own best self," was protesting her failure to follow through on promises made to herself (a "relative" whom she liked). He described her failure as being as serious as failing to honor an engagement for marriage. And he nailed down the challenge by picking out a warning to her from a dream had by Aaron, weeks before, in which he had seen that his wife should take Pluto water for her eliminations. She had concurred then, but now was careless, and her nursing baby suffered while she procrastinated.

The owner had rebuked the captain, in this dream, for sailing an unsteady course.

Long before, while pregnant before her miscarriage, Frances had also dreamed a contact with her best self, or soul, in this vivid anxiety dream:

> *Dreamed that I could never have a child—that none would ever come to me—that I would never give birth.*

Cayce assured her flatly that she would one day have a child (as in fact she did, but not the one she was carrying). He told her to forget any literal interpretation of the dream. Instead, he urged her to note the careful preparations she was making for motherhood: diet, physiotherapy, attitudes, exercise. These were her "highest service to the Maker, and to the one held dear," her husband. By reflection she might see why the dream took up these current preparations for birth as an emblem for the cleansings and disciplines she also needed, to prepare not for the baby, but for her own highest self, which needed to assume a larger place in her life. This was the birth that was in jeopardy, not her baby's. This was the child, the highest self, which would one day be her own greatest gift to her growing offspring.

A shipowner may trade in his ship for a new one.

It was part of the Cayce outlook that the soul reincarnates, taking successive voyages in lives on earth, of long or short duration. Each voyage is meant to enrich and enlarge the soul's total creativity in some specific way.

No single claim of Cayce's alienated so many people in his lifetime.

For years he had used his gift only for medical counsel. Then he had added not only counsel on oil wells, but even counsel on the affairs of nations. Through all of this psychic counseling, until he was forty-five years old, he had remained a psychological oddity—a marvel for some, an instance of self-delusion for others. But shortly before Frances and her husband had appeared in his life, he had commented, in trance, that people live on earth many times. From then on he was not only an oddity, but often someone to be shunned, by those who might otherwise have been drawn to him by his obvious gifts. Yet his psychic sources, at whatever cost to his personal popularity and self-esteem (for the idea of reincarnation was foreign to him as a Southern Protestant) insisted that such rebirth was a fact, to be observed as dispassionately as the broken legs which he described in medical counsel, or the stock trends that he described in business counsel, or the buried oil fields that he had located so brilliantly a few times in the past.

In the first reading that he gave to Frances, he told her, at her request, that in one of her past lives she had been a maid, an attendant, to Henrietta, the wife of Charles I of England. It had not been a particularly helpful life, for she had absorbed much of the spirit of court intrigue, especially from her mistress, and a style of "get even with you yet," when rejected or crossed. Cayce told her firmly that she would need above all in the present lifetime to learn not to act in spite or grudge—a warning he repeated many times. He saw it as the course of her soul to learn forgiveness and patience with others, while serving as Aaron's wife.

Her test eventually came, as it does to many, in marital conflict. Frances stayed with her husband eight years, but finally left him, not without some hints of the spirit of the English court. Her dreams showed her toying with the idea of a romance with an old boyfriend, to get even. But mostly her dreams urged her to patience and steadiness with her husband, when stresses came.

Frances' first dream drawing on past lives came as early as on her honeymoon, according to Cayce. Then, almost exactly a year later, came another, forewarning the blowup in her marriage several years afterwards:

> *My husband and I were on a boat, and there seemed much thundering or shooting and fighting. It ended with the boat being struck by lightning and the boiler exploding. It sank. We were blown up—killed.*

Cayce told her there would one day be conditions in her life (as in time there were), which would remind her of this dream, which he called a "vision" instead of a dream, because of its accuracy and depth. He told her that her subconscious was using the boat voyage as a symbol or emblem of the voyage of life. And he warned that there would indeed come a crisis in her passage through the affairs of her life, with turmoils and troubles. He spoke sternly to both husband and wife, saying that the warning of the vision had come to both, so "that the paths of each might be made more in accord one with the other." Yet he was not fatalistic, in speaking to Frances of this coming test of her ability to avoid spite or grudge. The "blowup" (Cayce insisted that dreams often dramatized figures of speech) could be followed by a "settling down" to a more perfect understanding by each marital partner, rather than by destruction.

The owner of the ship had called for preparations to meet a serious challenge.

In later years Frances had to meet once more such a challenge. Her son, like his father, was drawn into a marital tangle, and he suffered a nervous breakdown. This time she drew on deep resources of patience and fidelity, seeing him through in ways that won the admiration of friends, and could well have won from Cayce his cryptic remark of highest praise: "the entity gained, in that lifetime."

Three Levels in Dreaming

While Cayce described all of the above structures to Frances as operating in her dreams, he told her, as he did many others, that there are in effect only three levels in dreaming: the levels of body, mind, and spirit.

The body can initiate meaningful dreams, calling for physiological help through the assistance of the subconscious. Or it can produce meaningless dreams by sheer body chemistry acting on the nervous system, often from foods eaten, though sometimes from abnormal involvement of the endocrine glands, or through impaired circulation to the nervous system. He urged Frances to note that "there may be taken into the body physical . . . elements that produce hallucinations; or the activity . . . induced in the system," trying to handle troublesome foods or poisons "produces hallucinations, nightmares, or abortions to the mental forces of an individual."

Such dreams, or non-dreams, need to be distinguished from the more common dreams, he noted, which are initiated by mental or psychological activity.

Dreams of a primarily mental character are sometimes only conscious worries and concerns rehashed in the night.

But sheer worry dreams, Cayce said, are rare for those who work with their dreams. Usually, when conscious thought and effort are restaged in the night, they are shown in order to get a reaction from the subconscious, which proceeds to interpret conscious experience in new light, or to add its own ESP information from subconscious channels. As Cayce told Frances, some dreams are stimulated "from the mental mind of an entity, by deep study or thought" on a problem or an interest or a relationship. In such dreams, the outward "experiences of the individual entity are correlated" with inward structures and perspectives "through the subconscious forces of the entity—the latent forces of the entity—the hidden forces of the entity," which present the correlations "in a vision or a dream. Often these are as symbolic conditions, each representing a various phase to the mental development of the entity."

In yet other mental dreams, as Cayce saw them, the initiative lies more with the subconscious, warning or alerting the dreamer about something that has not yet entered his conscious experience, but is showing up on his internal radar because of the source on which he is headed.

To illustrate this latter kind of warning by the subconscious, Cayce singled out a dream of Frances that a close friend had committed suicide. The dream, said Cayce, accurately depicted a tendency in the friend which had passed. Such a dream developed by the "correlation between mentalities or subconscious entities" of the two dreamers, bringing "from one subconscious to another . . . actual existent conditions, either direct or indirect, to be acted upon" by loving care.

Finally, there are dreams from the dreamer's higher self, often given expression by a nameless voice in the dream, dreams from the superconscious, touching the Universal Forces. Cayce called such dreams "spiritual."

On her honeymoon, early in her recording of dreams, Frances heard just such a voice in a dream:

> *I dreamed I saw a woman, stretched on a bedspring, and the spring seemed to sway backward. I dreamed that something inside of me said, "Frances, you will awaken to something different," and I suddenly felt a smile on my face.*

In interpreting the dream, Cayce spoke explicitly of the "good pleasure" of "consummation" in the marriage, dramatized in the sexual imagery of the bed, postures, and swaying. He also spoke of the fullness of womanhood and personhood awakening in Frances as she gave herself in the sex act, and he described the voice that she had heard as "the superconscious," answering happily to the sexual experience and bringing a smile to her face in the dream. He gave her the impression that she was awakening at many levels at once—as many a bride has felt. Here, as in many other dreams, he noted that the typical function of the soul or of the superconscious in a dream was that of quickening or awakening to the dreamer to new inward potentials.

CHAPTER III. SOLVING PROBLEMS THROUGH DREAMS

Edgar Cayce encouraged Frances to interpret her own dreams.

Sometimes in his readings he quoted the saying, "Every tub must sit on its own bottom." It was this sort of self-reliance in Frances which he saw hinted in the following dream:

I was at the table with my husband and he was talking of my green water glasses. "Now just you keep quiet," I told him; "don't you criticize my glasses."

Although Cayce often told Frances that her dreams of others criticizing her were representations of her own sharp tongue, he took a different approach in commenting on this dream. The green, he said, was an emblem of healthy development—like the green in nature. She should therefore stick to what made sense to her "concept of creative forces." The glasses were vessels for what would be put into her body and life, whatever she chose to absorb and trust. He advised her, "Then do not care what others may say," just so what she saw and did squared with her own inner version of the "Creative Force" or God.

When Frances wanted to rely too heavily on dream messages from her dead mother, he again encouraged her to rely on herself. She reported to him the following: "Dreamed that my mother-in-law would tire of California and return home in six weeks." He told her that her perception was fairly accurate (as it proved to be), but when she asked if this perception had been guided from the next plane, he stressed that she had arrived at the dream conclusion from conscious reasoning in a dream state, rather than from any psychic experience. However, he encouraged her to develop within herself, by entering into periods of silence, the ability to achieve telepathic contact with those close to her, rather than seeking "spiritualistic conditions."

When she dreamed, more than a year before the 1929 stock crash, of the exact date on which she and her husband should sell their stocks, because of the "great changes" beginning then, he encouraged her to note how she could gain through such experiences whatever leads she needed for her daily activities.

Cayce invited Frances to do more than study dreams and dreaming. He pressed her to do more than study a psychic at work on her dreams. He coached her to interpret and use her own dreams on the problems of everyday life.

Problems with Relatives

There was, at the start of her dream-series, the problem she had with her relatives in her close-knit family of Southern Jews. They had shown not only the usual doubts about a northerner taking the flower of Southern womanhood, and some private family doubts over whether her husband's checkbook was as good as it looked. They had openly criticized his psychic interests. How was Frances to handle these relatives?

Even on her honeymoon trip, she dreamed of her family, as she reported to Cayce on successive days, in beginning her dream series.

> *I dreamed I saw my uncle stirring black coffee.*
>
> *I dreamed I was on a train riding back towards home in Mississippi.*
>
> *I dreamed I was on horseback and fell off. The same morning I dreamed of my father at home in Mississippi and awakened thinking of Cayce.*

Cayce told her that the first dream was of her uncle's actual views of her marriage—as mixed up as stirring black coffee which had no need to be stirred. The second dream, he told her, was a continuation of what she had been thinking before she dropped off into a nap (note that Cayce supplied this verifiable fact from hundreds of miles away, and several days later), which was that her actual train trip on a honeymoon was very different from a train trip she might be taking back home to her folks. The problem she was solving here, he said, was one of getting into perspective all that she was, as a bride, leaving behind. It was Frances' version of every bride's problem.

The third dream Cayce promptly corrected, as he often did, by telling the dreamer that she had left out a good deal of it. He then supplied the missing details for her to verify and study!

There had been not only the horse and rider, he said, but a vision of a roadway with various obstructions, and then an event to cause the horse to shy and the rider to fall.

This dream he treated as engaging the young bride at a much deeper level than the others—as an analyst might have guessed from the dynamic imagery of the horse, the presence of the father, and the hint of the awesome Cayce. But Cayce stressed no Oedipus problem in the dream, although it was likely that Frances' ties with her father were being brought to light by her having taken a man in marriage. Instead he saw the dream as continuing to handle the problem of the relatives' acceptance of her marriage, and of her husband's interests in psychic things.

He saw the horse as bringing a "messenger," a call that comes to everyone from his own best self. And he described her wonder at the things the rider had said, as well as her efforts to match the message with the views of people she held dear—such as her father. He saw the obstructions in the road as graphic dream images of the obstacles ahead in her new life path, and he warned her that the rider's falling off meant possible rejection of the message (which in fact occurred, as her dreams continued to warn, some five years later). Cayce spoke to Frances with unusual seriousness in interpreting this dream. He described her confronting of issues in sleep as "very, very good." Then he left her with the impression that in this dream she had gone beyond strategic problems of family harmony, to tackle the deep problem of what she was going to trust with her very life—what outlook, what faith, what principles. As always, he urged her to trust her own best judgment.

Frances' problems were not all so abstract. Still on her honeymoon, she sent to Cayce a sex dream that brought a different kind of response from him. She wrote:

> *I saw clearly a beautiful house on fire. The same night I dreamed a girl friend of mine was at a dinner table with many guests, including myself. It was back in Mississippi. She was making violent and demonstrative love to her old sweetheart of single days, who was seated next to her. The guests all criticized her for this.*

In interpreting this dream, Cayce departed from his usual method. Typically, he had the dream read aloud to him by his wife, while he was in his trance state, after which he would interpret it. But in this case he jumped into the interpretation after the first sentence, interrupting his wife, who was "conducting" the reading as hypnotists do. Ignoring the text of the dream, he proceeded to talk about it as though by ESP he had it all in mind—which in fact he did, as his comments showed.

Why the interruption? It seemed to occur, once in a while, when Cayce felt a special urgency about the subject of the reading he was about to give. Here the urgency showed in what he said to Frances.

He told her that the beautiful house on fire was but one of a series of dreams she had experienced, presenting something beautiful destroyed. In each case, he said, the destruction was represented by some symbol standing for misunderstanding with those of her household. Here it was fire, standing for *ire* in her dreams—a not uncommon dream symbol, he noted.

He was saying to a new bride just this: your dream is showing that your beautiful new relationship may well end in misunderstanding and bitter anger. Was Cayce justified in his warning? Eight years later the marriage ended in just this way.

Yet Cayce was no fatalist. "This should never begin," he said, as he urged the couple to begin working at once on understanding themselves and each other. And if the fire of rage should one day come between them, he added, they could come out of it better people, made more perfect or sound by passing through trial of fire, if they chose.

He stressed the importance of will power in each partner, and he traced its action in a tendency which the dream showed, for Frances to withhold a portion of herself in the marriage. She had repressed a part of the dream already, he pointed out, for he reminded her that only part of the front of the house was destroyed in the dream, while she had also seen blackened ruins in the rear.

What did the blackened ruins stand for? The answer lay in the violent love-making scene from earlier days, which followed in the dream, and brought criticism on the friend who was a stand-in for the dreamer.

Cayce spoke carefully of this portion of the dream, warning Frances that sexual improprieties could be expected to "shadow the life" ahead of her. In interpreting this dream (unlike another which Frances had much later, where her husband appeared in a doubtful light and left her to drown), Cayce spoke to Frances, herself. The trend of his comments was that she was keeping back part of her fantasies for her old sweetheart, and dwelling on these even during her honeymoon—and then finding herself accused by conscience pangs. He warned her, as he often warned others, that thoughts are deeds, with very real consequences. Apparently he was pointing to a chain of events familiar to psychiatrists: one partner in a marriage reserves a portion of himself from the marriage, but becomes so vulnerable to guilts as to be unable to forgive the other when the spouse in turn strays down similar paths. Was Cayce seeing something in Frances that might block reconciliation in later marital quarrels, and urging her to find the block for herself? Certainly he was not speaking of her activities, for she was freshly and happily married; nothing like an affair was in the picture.

Five months later he again interrupted a dream of Frances' being read to him:

My mother-in-law, my husband and I were living together in a house in Pennsylvania, and I heard much shooting and excitement. All of the windows of our house were open, and as it was raining and storming out, we rushed to close and lock them. Some terrible wild man seemed to be running through the town, shooting and causing great trouble, and the police were chasing him.

Here the unconscious Cayce interrupted the reading of the dream to tell the dreamer, as though she were in the room with him at Virginia Beach, instead of hundreds of miles away in New York, that "the large man, the bugaboo" was herself and her temper. Then he waited while the rest of the dream was read:

Conditions were chaotic and troublesome. We stopped the police to ask if they had caught this terrible person, and they answered, "Not yet."

Cayce responded at once that Frances should control herself, if this seemingly "terrible person" were to be "caught and conquered." To him the picture of her dream at work trying to solve the problem of her temper seemed completely clear—as it might to anyone living with Frances while she stormed about the house, making things chaotic and troublesome.

Not all of the problems which her dreams worked to solve were so serious. Some were as prosaic as her diet.

Problems of Health

She wanted to keep her girlish figure. It was important in her social circles, and of course carried sexual overtones to which both she and her husband were responsive. She dreamed of trying on clothes, and later, in pregnancy, she dreamed of her discouragement at being too large to go out for a formal evening. She frequently dieted, even though she was still in her early twenties, and not overweight. She cut out starches and sweets, as her strong will allowed her to do, and she created, according to Cayce, a problem for the economy of her body. Dreams were forthcoming to try to solve the problem.

Dreamed I said to my husband, "Now my cramps are all gone." He said, "That is fine." Then I awakened and all the pain was gone.

Cayce took a good deal of time with this little dream, showing her that the cramps she had actually been having in waking life, as well as in the dream, were caused by her reducing diet. He traced the effects of that diet, on digestion, eliminations, cell rebuilding, glandular operation, and circulation of the blood. Then he urged her to correct the diet as her own better judgment was already telling her. He also showed her how her figure-consciousness looked in her dreams when she told him a dream from the next night. "*Dreamed I saw J.B. and his sister. Something regarding looks.*" He reminded her that she viewed the man and his sister as people overconcerned with their looks. She had dreamed of them because to her own inner mind her superdieting for looks seemed just as unreasonable as they were.

A week later Frances dreamed further about her diet:

> *I was sitting at a table eating, but more than eating—I was packing it in. There was chocolate cake and all kinds of sweets and goodies—and I just had a great time eating it all up.*

Patiently Cayce explained that this, too, was a problem-solving dream for her body, and that she should eat more sweets, rather than damaging her body by her reducing diet. But he added that she should not take the dream literally, eating sweets only in moderation.

A year later she was still experimenting with diets to protect her figure, and she dreamed this:

> *It was raining starch, and I dreamed that I should go out in the rain of starch and put it on my side to ease the pain.*

Here again, said Cayce, the body was problem-solving through a dream. He explained at some length that the lack of starch in her diet was causing fermentation in organs on the right side of her body, producing pain, and that the lack of starch was not good for the foetus she was carrying, either.

The same night Frances had dreamed of a quite different kind of problem, which Cayce said showed her ESP warning her of coming distress:

> *I fainted on Fifth Avenue, falling to the street and knocking out several teeth. Leo seemed to have something to do with this.*

Somehow picking up the unknown Leo with his own clairvoyance, Cayce responded that this little dream came to warn her of coming distress from unkind things Leo was going to say about her. Then he added, as he often did in interpreting precognitive dreams, "Being forewarned, be prepared." He urged her to overlook and forgive the remarks when she heard them, not letting them "take root in the mind" as unkind jibes often do, leading to sharp words as hard to replace as teeth.

Quite another kind of associate was central in a dream drama which he said also called on Frances' ESP. She had lost a lovely jeweled pin that her mother had given her and she suspected that a servant had taken it. She dreamed:

> *Bob pointed out my lost pin to me as attached to my string of pearls. Upon investigating, I found it was another pin than that which my mother gave me, and not the one I wanted at all.*

To unravel this dream, Cayce had to read Frances' mind, focusing on her memory of how she had handled a suspected theft of clothing by one of her servants, some time back. Rather than accusing the servant and setting up her defenses, Frances had taken more positive steps to show the maid her own feelings and commitments about honesty, and the clothes were returned.

This time, however, Frances was impatient. The dream commented on her impatience. It showed her, Cayce said, that if she forced the issue with the present employee, a substitution would be made by the accused servant, to cover up the theft. Or else the servant would leave, and Frances would never regain the pin. Cayce urged her to do as she had done with the incident of the clothes, and as her own best judgment, he said, was already prompting her: to wait, to watch, to pray.

Then, typically, he pointed to an opportunity that lay before Frances—an opportunity to be to her maid a quiet kind of witness. He said the girl was ready to learn, if not too frightened. And he urged Frances to handle the incident so that she herself would not steal something from the thief more important than silver and gold: her self-respect, her chance to grow, her soul. He asked Frances to "put it into the heart, the mind" of employees and relatives about her "that the fear of the Lord—not law—is the beginning of wisdom."

By stressing the strength of the total orientation of a person, as greater than conscience and fear of punishment, and by trusting the relationship between Frances and her servant to bear good fruit, Cayce showed his own ultimate values. Such values inevitably affected all of his serious dream interpretation. In Cayce's view, nobody's problems were simply his own, and one function of dreams was to bring to light all the factors in a situation, as well as the most creative total solution.

Problems of Money

Frances held some stocks in her name, but it was her husband who did the investing—and the dreaming about investing. Still, she could not avoid being concerned with his concerns, and early in her marriage she had the following two dreams about stocks:

> *My husband and I were down South and saw thousands of little children learning to swim in a big lake. They were on some kind of rope contraption that went down at the sound of a whistle and thereby allowed them to swim in water up to their waists. I wondered how the rope thing worked, and what it was. Many older girls were also swimming.*

Cayce characterized the dream as one about the staple product of the South (where Frances had been reared): cotton. The big device was showing her the rise and fall of prices in the cotton market, in response to the whistle—call or demand—for cotton. The thousands of children represented new industries in the South, needing cotton, while the larger girls were the larger users and brokers, who affected the price-setting device the most. The water was there to show that the market affected real-life support and sustenance for many people.

He told Frances to take her cotton hunches to certain brokers outside the family (not to her husband, who was himself an experienced investor!); these would help her to use her dream tips to good advantage. Later, she came up with stock leads for her husband, as well:

> *My husband and I went to the L and N Railroad Station. He had missed his train. The first train had gone. I said to him, "You should never have missed that L and N train. You should watch the time better. You are too slow." He called a taxi to go to another railroad, but the taxi he called was a slow horse hack. Then I saw a fruit stand, and turning to my husband, said, "Buy me a piece of fruit."*

On this dream Cayce got right down to market details. Encouraging Frances to use such dreams for financial guidance, as he had encouraged her husband, Cayce pointed out that the dream was correct in showing that her husband had in fact missed a chance for a rise in L and N stock, on which he was short. He also pointed out that while Aaron could get out of his situation with L and N stock, as shown through the taxi, he couldn't make much money on the deal, as the slow hack indicated. The part about the fruit he called precognitive, insisting that the railroad and a fruit stock were soon to join in a combine that would affect their holdings. He urged Frances and her husband to be ready to buy when this occurred.

So Frances had her initiation into the world of market dreams, which were making so much money for her husband and his associates in the stock market.

When the great stock crash of 1929 began to come over the horizon, Frances and her husband both had clear and ample warnings, months in advance. The result was that her husband went through the crash and the early years of the Depression relatively unharmed, financially. He even went off to Europe at the trough to the Depression. It was his psychic guidance which he credited with saving his wealth, as it had earlier made him rich.

With the marriage break, Frances was left alone to support her son. In a few short years she had gone from modest means to exceptional wealth, and then to stringent need, with both of her parents dead. She needed every resource in her being.

One resource was her astonishing—and to her, at least, convincing—experience of reaching through death to her mother.

CHAPTER IV. ADVENTURING THROUGH DREAMS

It was typical for those who turned to Edgar Cayce for coaching on their dreams that they began to adventure through their nightly productions.

Many of their dreams focused on solving problems at all levels of their lives, as Frances saw.

But some of their dreams could only be called adventures. These were apparently bent on quickening hidden potentials in the dreamer—the second great function which Edgar Cayce saw in dreams.

Some of the systematic dreamers pursued mechanical inventions in dreams, such as a container for oil which made a great deal of money for one man. Some dreamed their way back into history. Some heard music, some investigated physiology in dreams. Three college students dreamed accurately of buried treasure. A housewife dreamed the answers to a contest on vitamins in Wonder Bread.

Most of the adventuring, however, went deeper. It led the dreamer into avenues which would broaden and transform his entire selfhood.

Transformation marked the adventuring that unfolded for Frances, in the four years that she sought dream counsel from Cayce. She explored, first through her dreams, and then in a few semi-waking experiences, the country of death.

Psychic Experiences in Dreams

Not all of Frances' psychic experiences in dreams had to do with the departed, with "discarnates," as psychic investigators call them. Some of her ESP went in quite other directions.

What appeared to be ESP took her back in time, into what Cayce called past lives. An early hint of this came in a dream six weeks after marriage. *"Dreamed my husband wasn't coming home any more, and I cried bitterly."* Cayce told her this dream imagery reached into her very soul. "The greater awakening of love, in self, for him, awakens those possibilities of the separate conditions." The deep stirrings which she was feeling as a young bride were also calling forth what Cayce called her karma: all the testings and questionings about men and love that lay locked in her inmost being.

The picture of real love bringing with it the possibility of real alienation was one which psychiatrists and poets alike would recognize, without the Cayce framework of reincarnation.

Despite such daunting episodes in her dreams, Frances was determined to develop her ESP, and her psyche seemed ready for some such awakening, if Cayce's interpretation of this early dream was correct: *"Dreamed I died."*

Here she was seeing, he said, the death of attachment to "physical forces," preoccupation with physical pleasures and diversions, so that her capacity for serious thought and creativity could be born. It was a dream of an ending to prepare for a beginning.

The same night she dreamed further of the awakening that was stirring in her, in response to the interests she saw in her husband and in Cayce:

> *Saw someone wearing a dress which I copied and wore. As I tried on the left sleeve it was very tight.*

They told me that is the way it should be. "Make me two, just like this," I said.

Cayce described her "putting on of apparel" as evidence of the awakening of her subconscious to put on its new potentials, especially for psychic experiences such as she might wish to copy from her husband and others. But he warned that when the dream showed her ordering two dresses, it showed a bit of her pride that had to be tamed.

His basic counsel was Biblical: "Seek and ye shall find. Knock and it shall be opened to you." Yet he noted that the dress would be tight, for she would have to yield a desire to show off to a "desire to show self acceptable to Him, the Giver of all good and perfect gifts, making manifest in word, action, and deed those lessons gathered." The psychic outreach she sought could not be ordered up like dresses, but "little by little, line upon line," as she learned to share her discoveries fruitfully with others. He continued in the same vein when she reported a further dream from the same night: *"Saw myself in various costumes."*

By reviewing this dream, he said, she could see herself gradually developing, gradually putting on exactly what she needed, at all levels, for her new awakening—spiritually, physically, mentally. And in his typical language for serious readings, he paraphrased two passages of the New Testament: "Put on the whole armor . . . those conditions that give of the spiritual kingdom. With this awakening"—awakening to the right kingdom first, he told her—"all physical, material will be added unto you" in gifts as helpful as her husband's and Cayce's gifts which she so admired.

It was not long before Frances began to show, in her dreams, an awakening of ESP talents that took two directions which stayed with her throughout her four years with Cayce. One direction was counsel on health matters, for herself and those close to her. The other was telepathy. These two gifts, together with her later capacity to reach through death to her discarnate mother, made up her special psychic profile—different from the profiles of others who sought dream counsel from Cayce.

The health tips in her dreams were simple. But they were

helpful. One of the first was a short dream: "Dreamed my husband's cold was worse." Cayce reminded her that she already had prescriptions to give him, and should do something about them.

Something more like ESP seemed evident in a portion of a later dream:

> *My husband and I went into a store and bought some candy, at which I said, "There you are bothering around buying candy. You know it is not good for you and that you should not eat it."*

It was time, Cayce told her, for her to guide and guard her husband in his appetite for sweets.

Aaron might well have listened to her, for a month before she had come up with a vivid dream for him that proved medically sound:

> *My ear seemed to trouble me and I said, "I know—it is a return of my old ear trouble." My ear pained me dreadfully. Yet it seemed to be my husband's ear—not mine.*

The last part of the dream, Cayce said, showed her the correct direction to look. For the dream was in fact a warning about an infection in her husband's Eustachian tube, leading to his ear. The dream had simply used her ear trouble to dramatize his need. Helpful as her dream was, Frances still had to ask Cayce which of her husband's ears was involved, and was told "the left"—as a doctor verified.

The same night Frances dreamed yet more strikingly of her brother-in-law's health:

> *Saw him get so terribly sick that I interfered, telling them that they should not permit a duplication of what happened in my mother's case.*

Cayce responded that she had correctly seen in the dream the gravity of letting her brother-in-law postpone medical aid, as her mother had fatally postponed it. But the interference, he said, was a depicting of helpful steps she had already taken in the family circle, which were beginning to bear fruit.

In six months she had an unforgettable experience of ESP at work in protecting the health of her loved ones. It seemed to her in her dream that her parents (who were by then both dead) appeared to her in a dream and were glad to see her. However, they expressed great concern:

> *They told me about my sister, that she had committed suicide, or killed herself.*

Cayce insisted that the dream was showing her the actual workings of her sister's mind, and that the sister was in fact carrying the thought of suicide, night and day.

Frances and her husband, alarmed, got on the phone at once to her sister, who broke down and admitted she was contemplating killing herself, as her father had done before her. Only the timeliness of the dream and the call, followed by long hours of counsel, saved the sister from death.

The ability to know, through dreams, the thoughts of others close to her, was not always so disturbing for Frances. She sent Cayce a brief note, along with other dreams, about a scene involving a favorite cousin: "*Dreamed my cousin William was married.*" Here she was having a correct premonition of his intentions, Cayce told her, and within the next three months she would receive a message that the marriage had happened. He suggested that she make a record of the dream, as he often suggested to others, first studying the outreach of the subconscious and its ESP. "Follow this," he said, "and it will be seen."

Cayce did not make clear whether Frances was sender or receiver in the delightful instance of dream telepathy which occurred when she was in early pregnancy. On the night of December 2, 1925, Frances' sister-in-law "*Dreamed Frances, my sister-in-law, had a new diamond flexible bracelet.*" She sent the dream to Cayce, as some of Frances' relatives were now doing. He told her that it represented Frances making preparations for motherhood, "for the greater bonds that bind self to the commendation of self, to the magnifying of spirit forces in earth plane." Cayce held a high view of motherhood, which could draw a helpful and talented soul into the earth plane for a new incarnation. To him pregnancy was fittingly symbolized by precious jewelry, and especially by jewelry which adorned the arms that would hold a baby.

On precisely the same night, Frances herself dreamed the following:

> *Dreamed I had bands on my fingers, which opened up into diamond flexible bracelets to my elbow. I was at home at the time, going to college, and was so excited I decided to stay home and not go to school. I was dressed in my red sweater and skirt. My mother urged me to remain home and celebrate the good fortune, and anyway I lost my schedule of my studies or hours, so could not go to college that day. I stayed home in excitement to enjoy the wonderful jewelry.*

To Frances, Cayce was even more detailed about the bracelets. They had first appeared as bands, he said, because of the bands on fingers that signify marital union. They had opened into arm bracelets because her marriage was opening "now, into that wonderful development, of that to occupy the entity in the arm full of jewels, as it were, from that union."

But now Cayce went beyond what he had told Frances' sister-in-law. To Frances he added that the full term of the baby would bring its birth in the middle of June, and that it would be a boy.

However, he warned her sternly that the birth might not take place, if she did not observe the necessary preparations and precautions, both mental and physical. (As a matter of fact, this pregnancy terminated in a miscarriage, two months later.) The dream about staying home from school and losing her schedule, he said, was showing her that she could be "lost in the maze of conditions or speculation" on motherhood. He urged her to take care of matters of diet and physiotherapy, as well as rest and freedom from worry, which he had outlined for her previously in a medical reading.

Frances was learning about ESP in dreams, though she had much to learn of motherhood.

Like her husband, Frances was fascinated by the question of whether human personality survived bodily death. In the early twenties there was still no systematic laboratory research on ESP. Indeed, Dr. J. B. Rhine, who was to invent the term, had not yet appeared on the scene of psychical research, as he was to do at Clark University, some years later, for a symposium with the famous psychologist MacDougall, and in the company of a young man destined to become dean of American psychologists, Gardner Murphy.

For Frances and her friends, psychic phenomena were almost synonymous with the question of life after death. Their interests followed the pattern of interests in the British-born Society for Psychical Research, which was then placing its sharpest attention on the investigation of mediums and spirit phenomena. The attention was not a morbid desire to retain contact with dead loved ones, but rather a desire to show that "mind" was an independent principle in man, something that survived his death and therefore deserved more attention during his lifetime than did "matter" and materialism. The search was basically for a philosophy of life, from which enthusiasts for psychic phenomena thought they could derive a new and compelling scheme of values for their world, still marked by the scars of the First World War.

Frances' interest in life beyond the grave was evident in a dream she had recalled early in her marriage, where the vehicle was of a type not uncommon for those who submitted their dreams to Cayce: a discussion dream, on a topic important to the dreamer.

> *I was in a discussion with Ted. I remember only a portion of this. Recall and interpret and explain to me so that my mind may grasp the significance and I may better understand the lesson intended. That I recall is as follows: Talking to Ted, I said, "Now, Ted, you see, death is not the grave as many people think. It is another phenomenized form of life."*

As he often did, Cayce began by telling the dreamer what part of her mind was at work, and how, in a particular dream. Here it was Frances' subconscious giving to her conscious mind, he said, lessons about the psychology of mental forces.

Then he went on to recall the dream for her, as she had asked:

> *This as the conversation, as we gain here. The discussion regarding that seen by the life in an individual, and the taking of same by any sudden action, see? And the discussion went into the particular condition regarding individuals' lives that were taken in heat of passion, or in war. And as the mental developed in discussion, we find the entity sees then in same something of that suggestion as was placed in waking life by one Ballentine, in the discussion of life after death. And the entity then sees, through subconscious forces, that death is as but the beginning of another form of phenomenized force, in the perspective of the earth's plane.*

The term "phenomenized" was one much used by Frances' husband at the time, to suggest that one life force was at work behind the phenomena in which a person expressed his being, whether in a "third-dimensional" earthly body or a different "fourth-dimensional" form beyond the grave.

Cayce continued his report by emphasizing, as he often did, that post-death existence could not be grasped rationally and logically, but had to be experienced by psychic attunement which could put an earthly person *en rapport* with that other state.

> *And may not be understood by the third dimension mind from third dimension analysis, but must be seen from that fourth dimension force as may be experienced by an entity gaining the access to same by development (psychically and spiritually) in the physical plane, through the mental processes of an entity.*

He added that Francis was gaining the ability for just such an attunement. Then he went on to explain further, as she had asked.

We see in the physical world the condition (of death) in every form of life. As is taken here: we find in a grain of corn or wheat that germ that, set in motion through its natural process with Mother Earth and the elements about same, brings forth corn after its kind, see? The kind and the germ being of a spiritual nature. The husk or corn, and the natural or physical condition of it, being physical forces, see? Then, as the corn dies, the process is as the growth is seen (in the dream) in that as expressed to the entity. And the entity expressing same, see? That death is not as commonly viewed, is not that of the passing away, or becoming a non-entity.

Cayce was agreeing with the comments Frances had made in her dream, where she identified life beyond death as "another phenomenized form" of the life force. The body would be left behind like the husk of a seed, and something new would come forth from its germ. Cayce was, however, stressing something he never failed to underscore in discussions of life beyond death, the matter of the *kind* or quality of post-death existence that a person was building in his earthly life. This was the essential *spiritual* question, he suggested to Frances, the question of the spirit or trend or quality of a person's being—not just his enduring or surviving. To be sure, the husk would be discarded. But what would be the pattern of the emergent germ?

Frances had no idea that her dreams of life beyond death were serving a purpose other than developing her intellectual interests. But within a month and a half her mother, now well, would be dead of cancer. And within a year and a half her father would be dead by his own hand, an instance of the process about which Frances was dreaming: "lives that were taken in the heat of passion." Slowly her dreams seemed to be preparing her. A dream which came two weeks later was one which Cayce said specifically was *not* a foreboding.

Dreamed my father died. It must have been in the near future, because my mother was still limping from a recent accident in which her foot was hurt.

The dreaming of the father's death, he said, was simply an echo of her conscious concern over his diabetic condition. To help her, he spelled out for her father a correct diet, physiotherapy manipulations, and a detailed prescription for a four-part tonic to be taken three to four times daily. Regarding the mother in the dream, Cayce came up with a contrasting interpretation. Frances' letters to her mother were hurting her feelings, "crippling" her, so to speak, and Frances should use "more care in the manner and way in which the communications are addressed to the mother."

But the dream which came two weeks later was of a different order. By then Frances' mother was in the hospital for surgery on her eye, which revealed a malignant growth.

> *Dreamed that my sister and myself were on my bed with our mother. Mother was unconscious. Both my sister and myself were crying and saying, "Don't leave us!" Suddenly our mother awakened and started to talk out loud, very loud, but it didn't seem like our mother talking at all.*

Worried, Frances asked whether the dream meant that her mother would recover or would not recover. Cayce replied that it did not mean either, but was instead a lesson from the subconscious, giving "possibilities of actual conditions that might be existent in the physical forces" of her mother. Frances' subconscious was showing her the truth of "the soul liveth," as he put it, and Frances was to study the dream, in order to "gain the strength to bear with the weaknesses of the heir of fleshly conditions," or to bear death.

Reassuring her, Cayce turned to what her husband had dreamed, but not reported to him, the same night—Aaron had seen Frances weeping. The important point was not death-loss, Cayce said, but was the lowly spirit of the weeping, in which Frances could be seen emptying herself of physical understanding, in order to receive a grasp of spiritual conditions as they really stood with her mother.

Meantime, Frances' mother was having her own dreams in the hospital, one of which she asked Frances to send to Cayce for interpretation.

I saw all my children, husband, and even my cook and maids—all with whom I am associated—I saw them as Dead.

Cayce told the sick mother that in this dream her subconscious was viewing from a superconscious perspective, how far each person in the dream fully comprehended the relations between earthly and post-death life. (Such a survey dream, wherein the dreamer explored the attitudes of each participant, was a not uncommon type of dream, in the Cayce view.) She saw the individuals as dead, he reported, because they would each have to go through a kind of "death" to false attitudes and convictions, if they were correctly to understand what she was going through in her own extremity.

Her opportunity, then, lay in what she could show them in the manner of her own dying (he called it what "the physical is passing through"). She could be an example of real strength of spirit, which might help each of her loved ones to grow towards "the full awakening to each," by the dying to live again which must take place in each—not just bodily but totally, existentially. By such dying or death needed for each, he added, "the whole force of the life is meant, see?"

The dreams that came to Frances seemed to continue to prepare her for the loss she dreaded.

I saw handwriting on the wall, with "Well." I didn't understand and went back to sleep and saw myself in a blue and white dress. I was kneeling down on my knees before the doctor and he patted me on the head, and I said, "Through you and God Almighty has our mother been spared to us"; and then he said, "Let us pray again. . . ."

At about this time Frances' mother did make a temporary recovery, even leaving the hospital for a while. Later, Cayce said that the respite had been brought almost entirely by prayer. But he must have had little doubt of the eventual outcome, for he interpreted the dream, again, as one preparing Frances to accept death. Under the existing conditions, he said, the dream was showing Frances herself that "there is only then for the entity to put self into the hands of the Giver of all good and perfect gifts. For in choosing the physician"—or "The Physician"—this would be "the best, then, for self, and for the good of the mother." The blue and the white of her dress he interpreted as he did the same colors elsewhere under similar dream conditions, as truth and purity—this time in her prayer and supplication. The handwriting she had seen, he said, was like that of Biblical times, and it meant "All is well"—not necessarily medically, but in the more perfect understanding of death that could come to Frances if she put her trust where it belonged. It was the answer to her prayer, but in God's terms, not hers.

Cayce was showing Frances, as he did many others, that dreams were a natural and appropriate vehicle in which the answers to prayer might be given.

Later the same night Frances had her first dream of the sort that Cayce often called a vision, because of its strong effect on the dreamer and its classic symbolic language.

> *I saw a man with a gray beard, dressed in pure white like a sheep. It so impressed me that I said, "I can't believe it." I saw him pull my mother by the arm out into the light.*

Such dreams or visions always had a direct effect on Cayce as he spoke of them, calling forth from him the Biblical imagery in which his own faith was held. Though Frances' mother was Jewish, Cayce explained the vision in Christian terms:

> *This, as we see, is presenting to the dreamer that as is none other but the Lamb, the Redeemer. For as is given (in scripture), through Him is there gained access to that throne of mercy, grace and pardon. And in complying with those ways that He taught, as is set through His words, may we all be led into the light, see? That the wool, though red like crimson, shall be white, in His obedience, His ways, His precepts. And these, as we see, bring all to that great white Light, see?*

There was no question to Cayce but that Frances' mother had lived the kind of life which would give real quality to that part of her that survived bodily death, and would place her in living touch with the highest spirituality Cayce knew.

Then, a little over a month before her mother died, Frances had her final warning dream.

> *My mother was well and to be married and all were celebrating. I was sad because I could not join in the merry-making, because I knew she had to be operated on again, and would die. Also, I was disappointed because I was not invited to her wedding.*

As it turned out, her mother did require another and unexpected operation, after this dream, and died from it.

In interpreting the dream, Cayce acknowledged the sadness, born of what Frances correctly knew was happening to her mother. Yet he insisted, "The mother is well—will be well." Here he echoed the imagery of the dream, with its note of joy and of a very special turning point coming to the mother. But he added that the mother's welfare lay "not through an operation, but through the applications of spiritual forces that may be awakened in the individual." Frances' mother was awakening to the next plane of her existence, and it was an occasion for merrymaking, despite Frances' inevitable sadness that she would not be invited along. Patiently, Cayce urged Frances to review the seemingly impossible drama of the dream, in order to catch the spiritual lesson through her own awakening, not judging from physical reasoning alone.

Clearly, if survival of death were a fact, then dreams which anticipated death for someone who had lived long and well could not be limited to imagery of grief, real as the sorrow of survivors might be. Nothing less than a wedding could set forth the event!

Dreaming through the Barrier of Death

On the night after her mother died, Frances had a peculiarly vivid dream of an old friend of her mother's, who had died three weeks previously in another part of the country, but who had quite slipped her thoughts in her anxieties over her mother.

I heard a voice that I recognized as our old friend from Mississippi, who loved me dearly as a child, yet whom I have not seen in two or three years. The impression of her talking to me was very pronounced, and for a while I did not see her figure, yet I felt that she was with Mother at the hospital, as Mother changed from this earthly consciousness to the other. She was there as the transition was made, and was now with Mother as she said to me, "Your mother is as happy as ever." More she told me about Mother which I can't remember. Recall and explain to me, please.

Cayce assured Frances that she was being shown in her dream "what is meant by the life other than the physical." Recalling the Biblical phrase, "As the tree falls, so shall it lie," he pointed out how natural it was for someone who had loved her mother in life to continue that same love in the next plane, by helping her mother through the events of death.

Frances should take strength, he said, from the knowledge that the dream had explicitly given her, of the companionship her mother was finding. Emphatically he told her. "She is *well, happy* and *free,* from the care as is given in earth's plane." Frances could attune herself to psychically grasp the facts, if only she would not condemn herself for whatever she felt she had failed to do for her mother—a condemning which Cayce said brought needless sorrow to Frances.

Her dream was showing Frances in the clearest terms how friendship and love rule death as well as life. Through the dream experience, which was not symbolic but literal, Frances could know for sure, "*not alone* does the mother go out; not alone in that unseen world; yet with that same care, that same love (which she knew on earth), raised to a better *understanding* of the forces as are manifested" in life and in death.

When Frances asked whether someone such as her mother's friend would actually guide a dying person, Cayce answered that it was exactly this way, and only lack of understanding prevented the living from knowing it. He reminded Frances of two Biblical sayings as he tried to quicken her to a realization of what seemed to his vision to be unshakably true: "Lo, I am with thee" and "Though I walk through the valley of the shadow of death, my spirit shall guide thee."

Frances had experienced something else on the night her mother died. It was just a voice speaking to her quietly in her sleep, which said, *"Your mother is alive and happy."* But by then she knew that Cayce interpreted this kind of voice as her own higher self, her own soul, speaking to her in her dreams. And this was exactly the interpretation he stressed, in the questions and answers that followed, with an urgency which showed Cayce himself caught up in Frances' adventure into the land of death. He spoke with strong feeling: "Your mother *is* alive and happy." Then he contained himself and returned to a more objective style of speech:

> *The entity may know that all force (both within and without the person) goes to show, to prove, to bring to the consciousness of the entity, that as ye live in Him, ye shall be made alive in Him at death! For there is no death. Only the transition from the physical to the spiritual plane. Then, as the birth into the physical is given as the time of the new life, just so, then, in physical (death seen properly) is the birth into the spiritual.*

Frances had dreamed of her mother's death as a wedding. Cayce was telling her it was a birthday, too!

She asked a question: "Then, does my mother see me and love me as ever? Cayce answered swiftly: "Sees thee and loves thee as ever. Just as those forces were manifest in the physical world." It was up to Frances, he said, how much reality that love would have, as she "entertains and desires, and places self in that (inward) attunement with those desires of that entity (the mother), the love exists—in that far, in that manner, see? For in spirit all sham is laid aside." The mother's love was there, he said. How free was Frances of guilt and grief and fear, so that she could accept it and return it?

Frances asked further, "Then, does she try to tell me, 'I am alive and happy'?"

Cayce's answer was clear, but again emphasized Frances' own role, and the source of the voice as her own: "*Tells* the entity 'I am alive and happy,' when entity will *attune* self to that at-oneness." He was making the proper vehicle of communication a deep inward turning in a spirit of prayer—not a seance.

Frances went on, somewhat hesitantly. "I feel her with me, particularly as I kissed her clay body—I felt she knew and responded—but did she, or do I fool myself?"

Cayce replied swiftly, telling Frances that in the same manner as she had "poured out self" to her mother, "the response came." "No, not fooling self," he went on, "for the soul liveth, and is at peace, and would that the daughter know that it liveth."

Then he turned again to Biblical passages, giving them an immediacy that often showed in his readings: "As has been given, 'In my Father's house are many mansions; were it not so, I would have told you' and 'I go to prepare a place for you, that where *I am,* there *ye* may be also.' This is as applicable to the daughter in this hour as was given by the Redeemer to those gathered about Him." He continued, "For as we entities in the physical plane prepare that at-oneness (which could unite us with those in another plane), it is as He gave: 'Even as I be lifted up, I will draw *all* men unto me.' "

The doorway through death, Cayce was saying, lay in inward attunement to the One who could properly open it for communication between the living and the dead. He turned back to a teaching of Moses to develop the same theme once more: communication with the dead was not primarily to be found through an intermediary like Cayce, but in the dreamer's own inward experience.

> *"Say not to thyself, who shall descend into depths to bring him up, or who shall fly into the heavens to bring him down, for the spirit of peace, truth, and love, is within thine own heart." As the spirit of oneself gives that (proper) attunement, there may be an at-oneness with those spirits in that other sphere, that each may know, may understand, may gather, that truth that makes one free.*

Frances had, in Cayce's view, been given a memorable quickening on the night of her mother's death.

One more dream, from that same night, summed up what had happened to her, in simple but forceful imagery.

I saw an animal crawling over the ground, just sort of semiconscious, in a condition of half gray dawn.

Frances was, he said, seeing herself. She was seeing herself awakening. She was becoming conscious, however slowly, of the indwelling of the spirit within her—a spirit which could bear witness to the truth "of the Spirit of that One that gives and takes, and gives and takes—that we may become (alike through life and through death) one with Him."

The function of dreams, Cayce had told Frances many times, was not alone to solve problems. It was also to awaken the dreamer to his full stature as a person.

Frances was waking up.

Contact with the Dead

It was not long before the figure of Frances' mother began to appear in her dreams. Usually the figure came to further the inward stirrings that were occurring to Frances as a young woman. Occasionally it helped her with practical problems as well.

One of Frances' first needs was to handle the grief which she felt over not insisting that her mother receive precisely the medical care that Cayce had prescribed. The care had included (as was usual for Cayce in dealing with cancer patients) the application of a certain kind of ultra-violet light. It was a treatment which the doctor had neither understood nor sanctioned.

A few nights after her mother's death, Frances dreamed:

Saw my mother with two lamps shining on the back of her neck. The lamps were administered by Dr. K.

This dream was not, Cayce said, a message to Frances from her mother. It was simply her own subsconscious, trying to get at the truth of the medical situation. It was showing her exactly how the blood would have been affected, to bring relief to her mother. But, Cayce insisted, the point of the dream was not to bring her any sort of self-condemnation—just understanding, should she again someday have to make comparable judgments about doctors and treatments. She must understand that the treatment would not have saved her mother's life in any case, only stayed it awhile, and brought her some relief.

Several months later Frances again dreamed of her mother. Again Cayce said it was not a communication from her mother.

This dream was very clear and seemed so realistic that my mind upon awakening remembered it and was impressed. I seemed about to have a baby, and was very sick—vomiting, etc. My mother was there and said it must be that I was sick, not pregnant. I asked for the doctor to be called, which my mother did. I seemed to have some sort of miscarriage—at any rate it ended that I was not pregnant but my sickness came from something else entirely, as the doctor informed me.

This dream, said Cayce, came because it was time for her to conceive again, to fulfill her vocation of motherhood—*symbolized* by the appearance of her mother in the dream. She would have to face the fears left by her miscarriage, and set about getting her body in shape for pregnancy. If she did so, she need have no fear of losing the child (she did not lose the baby this time), for as the dream showed, her problems lay only in her general health, not in her capacity for childbearing as such.

But Frances was hesitant. The disappointments of her miscarriage and her mother's death were still vivid to her, and she seemed to have repressed the whole question of pregnancy as well as put off getting the proper medical care. Then there came the first dream which indicated that her mother's help was available.

I was paralyzed. I called to my mother and was frightened. Parts of me seemed to break or burst and I could not check this process, although I tried to desperately. Finally I suffered so that I wished to die.

Cayce told her bluntly that her dream showed her mental development at a standstill. She was letting herself become paralyzed as a person. The dream was not about her body, but about her consciousness, her growth as a person. She was going to have to quit fighting and denying the call to further development heard in her inner being—especially the call to motherhood. Then he added that she should note how in the dream "there is the call to that consciousness to whom . . . the body turns for the instruction, see?" It was her first hint that her mother could assume a helping role, in her dreams.

She did become pregnant. She did begin on the program of medical care which Cayce urged for her. Then she discontinued it, despite a constant backache. Aaron was frantic. Later he wrote to Cayce:

I tried to persuade her, and she grew angry with me . . . Night before last I prayed that (her mother), the psychic activity in the One Mind who was aware of the condition in her daughter's psyche, might appear and prevail upon her to do that which was best for herself and the forming child . . . I asked the Lord to join with me in this endeavor to better facilitate His creation. The wonderful response came as the dream indicates.

Frances dreamed that very night her first vivid contact with her mother.

My mother appeared to me. I saw her distinctly. She said to me, "You should go to the doctor. You ought to be ashamed of yourself! If Aaron wants you to go to the doctor, you should go."

The dream required little interpretation. Aaron reported that the effect of the dream on Frances had been so telling that "all the king's horses and all the king's men couldn't keep her away from the doctor." When Frances asked how her longing for her mother and her husband's prayer had contributed to the experience, Cayce answered: "The prayers of the rightcous shall save many. 'Where two or three are joined together in one purpose, I am in the midst of same.' " The combination of the action of all, including the mother, had made the attunement possible.

Within two weeks Frances began to have frequent dreams in which her mother was present, either as an actor in a drama (which Cayce said was sometimes Frances dreaming under the influence of her mother and sometimes just dreaming of what her mother represented to her), or as a vivid personage, herself (which Cayce said was literally her mother, communicating with her).

The dreams were not an obsession with Frances. They were mixed in, from the first, with dreams such as she had been dreaming all along—a dream about trouble with her gums (which Cayce traced to circulatory problems in with her pregnancy), and a dream of lightning striking her (which Cayce said was a depicting of some of the fears current in her pregnancy), and a dream of success for the book her husband was writing (which Cayce said was an authentic preview of its potential).

Guidance from the Dead in Dreams

It was a practical matter which next brought the mother and her "guiding forces," as Cayce called them, into a dream:

> *I was sick in a hospital and my mother was with me. It was either to have my baby or that I had a miscarriage again. Something wrong with my busts, and my mother said it should be remedied.*

Nothing was physically wrong with Frances, according to Cayce. The dream came only to alert her to a need of the forthcoming child: it should be nursed at the breast, not bottle-fed.

A few nights later Frances had another dream that combined her mother's aid with Frances' own bent towards medical ESP (it is perhaps significant that concern for medical care was a feature of Frances' entire life: after her divorce she became a nurse). Her dream began:

My mother appeared to me. She said to me: "I am alive."

Here Cayce interrupted with a note of happy urgency: "She is alive." The dream continued with the mother speaking further:

"Something is wrong with your sister's leg, or shoulder." (Or both—I don't clearly remember.) "She ought to see a doctor about it."

Here, Cayce said, Frances could see her mother being mother to her whole household, through Frances' mind. For Frances' subconscious, when she was asleep, had been "in at-onement with the mother and the sister." There was in fact, Cayce said, a medical problem in the sister's limbs, an auto-intoxication through poisons from the system. The sister should be warned to seek medical care. And the cure, Cayce added, would involve an increase in her eliminations.

Both Frances and Aaron were immensely interested in this experience, which proved to have a sound medical basis—although one of which the sister was not conscious at the time of the dream. Their sense of high adventure in cooperation with the dead was apparent in their correspondence with Cayce.

Two months later there came another experience of the mother which was so vivid that it woke Frances up and sent her scurrying to her husband's bed.

I dreamed of the play we saw . . . and then experienced my mother's presence right in my room with me. Her presence was so real, so pronounced and so close to me, the vision of her being there so vivid, that I jumped up in fright and ran from my bed into Aaron's.

But the dream experiences of the mother kept coming. One was a warning that an aunt was in a state of mind that made her accident-prone; it prompted Frances to visit her. Another was a warning regarding the danger of pneumonia to a much older aunt.

Then Frances reported a further set of dreams involving her mother and herself. These were not on practical matters at all, but on Frances' own depth and growth as a person, said Cayce.

> *I beheld my mother. She was displeased with me because I was going out to theatres, etc. She said, "The least you could have done for me was to keep mourning for one year."*

This was not a message from the mother, said Cayce, but Frances' own best self reviewing her whole relation with her mother. It was not underscoring a duty (such as the Jewish custom of a year of *kaddish*, or prayers of mourning), but an orientation. For the experiences Frances had been through since her mother's death, "the appearances, the nearness, the feeling of the presence in the room, the full conditions (of concern and aid) as have been presented," were bringing out the best in Frances. Around these experiences, and the study of them, were developing a new and genuine spirituality which was native to Frances and should be cherished—even as one cherishes the memory of a loved-one dead.

The other dream made the point in a different way:

> *Dreamed I was insane—my mind gone and my reason unbalanced. My mother was there and was having an awful time with me.*

Here again, Cayce indicated, Frances could see how important to her total maturity were the awakenings of meaning and perspective coming to her from "the essence of the presence of the mother." The dream was showing Frances something she already knew about herself: "that there have been moments when the entity (Frances), in its attempting to belittle elements as pertaining to a spiritual understanding, has put its mentality into an unbalanced condition . . . creating barriers that have been hard to break, hard to be understood, even by self." The times she had mocked Aaron for his studies, since her miscarriage and her mother's death, were telling on her. She must, Cayce said, "keep self mentally, morally, physically, spiritually in that at-onement with the universal forces that give the better understanding to each and every entity."

Frances next dream of her mother came through a correlation of Frances' mind and her mother's, as Cayce described it. The dream was memorable, both for its startling precognitive detail and for the bit of Jewish folk-mannerism used by her mother in the dream, giving it a tang of reality.

I dreamed of my baby. It was just born and weighed eleven pounds and two ounces. It had blue eyes and blond hair, and was a boy. It had, however, a Jewish nose that I didn't like. I said to my mother, who was there: "It looks kikish—too Jewish." My mother, however, bit her finger in characteristic fashion and beamed upon the baby. She said it was grand.

Frances was only five months pregnant, yet her dream of the final features of the baby was substantially accurate, according to Cayce. He assured her that he would be a boy, that he would be blond, that his eyes would be blue; his weight, however, would be closer to nine pounds. (In every detail Cayce proved correct, when the baby was born.) Regarding the nose, Frances was only partly right, he said, for while there would be something of a Jewish nose, his features would be even and attractive (as they were). This part of the dream, he added, had come to underscore to the mother the boy's potential life work of religious teaching to his own people, and to prepare her for it (as a young man her son did indeed begin to turn towards the vocation of a rabbi, but crisis and illness intervened).

Dream material from later the same night underscored the same themes, and in addition previewed the delivery—a time which proved to be one of the highlights of Frances' entire adventure with her mother.

I was on the obstetrical table, my mother there as before. I had a very easy time—so easy I could even get up and walk after the baby was delivered. I looked at my baby. It was then one or two days old as before, but instead of being partially homely it appeared to be a beautiful child with light hair, blue eyes and a healthy baby. It got up from the crib and came to me and said: "Here, I have a letter for you, Momsy!"

The dream came to urge Frances to make every preparation for the delivery in diet and rest and physiotherapy. And the part about the letter was just another way of saying that the baby could grow into a man with a special message to give.

Frances went right on dreaming during the months until the baby came. She dreamed of her husband's moneymaking, of the mental illness of a friend, of travel during pregnancy, of her husband's plans to join with others in building a hospital at Virginia Beach where Cayce's work could be better used and studied. She dreamed of her husband's talkativeness, of her own triviality, of the illness of her relatives. But she did not dream further of her mother.

Still fearful about the birth, she kept in close touch with Cayce. In January, he told her that the birth would be normal, and would come between March twenty-eighth and April sixth. It came April fourth. A few days before delivery, he told her all was well, and that the baby would arrive within ninety-six hours. It came in seventy-two.

With the baby came an unforgettable experience of Frances' mother.

Contact with the Dead beyond Dreams

What happened was best told in a letter to Cayce from Aaron:

Now, as great an objective demonstration of spirit communication that I have ever seen or hope to witness occurred this afternoon between Frances and her mother, as I was holding her hand. It also indicates that anesthetic (as pointed out by Ousepensky) makes the mind subject, or opens it subconsciously, to communication. Frances' pains were so bad that they gave her an ether enema and it doped her. Hazily, she said to me: "My mother is with me. She has been with me since this morning. See, she is right there!" Then Frances pointed to the other side of the bed from which I was sitting, and indicating a little above her head, again said: "My mother is right there."

"What is she saying?" I asked.

"She is saying," replied Frances clearly and precisely, "not to worry—that everything is coming out all right!"

"How do you know she is here with you?" I asked.

"I feel her—I see her—she is praying for me—she is here right with me—right there," and again Frances pointed her hand to the same exact location.

Aaron went on, in his letter.

Now I ask you, have you ever heard of anything so wonderful? Poor little kid; only her sister of her own kin with her, having lost her mother comparatively recently, longing for her on this day of suffering more than ever, feels and knows that her loved one is with her and hears from her. Her heart lonesome for that mother, bravely not complaining of her heartache, reaches for the mother, and glory be to the Almighty she reaches out not in vain!

I tell you, when I came out and told five grown folks about this, including my very practical mother, every one of them cried like babies. Darn it, I am bawling as I write this. It sort of has me in a daze—I don't know just how to be grateful enough or what to do. It's so wonderful, so definite, so precise, so beautiful, that it is far beyond me. In some small way I hope to come somewhere near to appreciating such an experience, for I know it is bewildering and beyond me above and mightier than poor little me.

Who cares for the opinions of those who call spirit communication bunk? What do their opinions amount to, anyway? What weight have they in the constructive field of knowledge-building?

A little pain-wracked body, harboring a lonesome and aching heart, receives not only a response from the spirit mother that comforts the heart, but actually aids, encourages and sustains the physical strength of this body and does it in no uncertain manner. Is this, then, impractical? Is it illusionary? Well, then, make the most of it—I intend to in my lifetime, believe me!

This is what I was trying to tell you over the phone, and I'm glad I couldn't. Must close and go to bed, as I am dead tired.

He asked Cayce to review the experience in a reading, explaining how it had all happened.

Evidently the force of the experience touched something in Cayce, himself, for during his reading there occurred something quite rare in his trances. Five different discarnates spoke through him—including the mother, herself. One was purportedly a well-known philosopher. Two were strangers to both Cayce and the dreamer. One was a family friend of Cayce's. Each spoke briefly and added a viewpoint on what had happened in the hospital; all were in agreement that the experience had been genuine.

Three confirmed what Aaron had suspected, that he, too, had experienced the mother in the hospital room, though in a different kind of psychic experience than Frances had been through. His had been an inner attunement, with no form or voice evident—only "an inner consciousness of the presence of another being." Frances, on the other hand, had found her "sensuous faculties" quickened in the experience, until the mother was "seen, felt, heard, known, by the subjugated consciousness," under drugs.

The unusual Cayce reading was not an instance of what investigators call "direct voice" mediumship (which happened to him in trance even more rarely), but one in which he was using his own language and consciousness to try to communicate the sense of what he felt another person, a discarnate, was saying.

When Cayce drew near to the end of the reading, the message came, as Aaron had hoped it would, from Frances' mother. Cayce expressed it in these words: "To Frances I have come, in that certain way that makes known the life after death." Then Cayce added his own assurance:

And the willingness of the mother is to ever be present, in the mental attitude of the daughter, to shield every thought, every care.

The final words were again from the mother, as Cayce felt them. Not surprisingly, in the light of the views that Cayce and the dreamers held, there was a reference to reincarnation. "Be thou faithful, then, in those lessons I have given to you; be faithful to Aaron, and to the baby—who comes from among us, and whom I have known before."

The reading was exciting for Frances. But she was not relying on it to carry the whole weight of assurance that she and her mother were reaching one another. Something else had happened in the hospital, a few days after the birth, which she reported to Cayce. She had been dozing when this occurred:

Heard a rapping noise or knocks. I said to myself: "That is my mother." I sat up in bed to listen for the noise, and heard nothing. Again dozing, I heard the knocks, and again recognized them as being my mother.

This was an authentic experience, according to Cayce, coming to her not as a novelty but to stimulate her to a better awareness of the nature of love, between those alive or dead—"the living from plane to plane"—however encrusted love might become in the life and action of each. It had been the same kind of experience, he reminded her, that her husband had undergone when he had felt the bed trembling, months ago, while at her mother's side shortly after she died. The two of them, Frances and Aaron, should "keep these things—pondering them in the heart."

Now there began the final chapter in Frances' dreams of

her mother. There was still to be a full year of varied experiences in dreams, before Frances' coaching by Cayce camc to an end.

Varieties of Dream Sharing with the Dead

A motif that reached deeply into Frances' makeup, according to Cayce, appeared in the next dream where her mother appeared. In the dream, as often, Frances saw male intruders—but this time they did her no harm. While still in the hospital with her baby, she dreamed:

> *My mother and I were in our old house in Mississippi, where we lived when I was a little girl. Mother and I were always afraid, and on this occasion heard men enter the house. Upon going to investigate, we found three men had broken in—but not to steal but to enquire about leaving liquor at our house. They said that they would give us several days to think it over and give our decision.*

The heart of this dream, Cayce told her, was the shift from the theme of illegality—both of the breaking-in and the liquor (these were Prohibition days), to the theme of considerateness and helpfulness. It was, he said, a dramatization of Frances' own opportunity, now begun in the arrival of her son, to move from "the letter of the law" to "the law of grace."

The locale of the home showed her the seriousness of the dream, he suggested, for it represented—as he often said of loved childhood homes—her spiritual home, her "indwelling." How was it to be entered? As a lawbreaker, bringing on suffering and punishment? Or in the way of the mother, as a way of faith, and of giving to others?

Cayce had told Frances before that in past lives she had been a woman of much beauty, as lovely as Helen of Troy. Like Helen, she had been unfaithful, and willing to use her charms to get men to do her will. The result was that she entered this life with a deep fear of men—that they in turn would be unfaithful and would misuse her; this was the repeated dream motif of male intruders and pursuers.

If she were to live under "the letter of the law," she would have to experience from men the same hardship she had brought upon them, until her soul learned the lesson and she entered her "spiritual home" wiser, as a chastened lawbreaker. (In point of fact, Frances did find herself in deep distress with men, a few years later, when she divorced her husband. For a while she also drank heavily, as Cayce warned her this dream had indicated.)

But her relation with the baby was presenting her with "the way of escape," he said, if she wished to choose it. By giving generously to this man-child, and to his father, she could quiet forever her own fears and hates, born of her own misdoings. On this course, she would come under "the law of grace, the law of mercy," and whatever events developed for her, she could meet them without fear or inner suffering. (Long after the divorce, when her son was a grown man and a troubled man, Frances nursed him and cared for him, faithfully, in just this way—fulfilling then the way of loving service that she could not earlier find in her heart for Aaron.)

In Cayce's view, this dream, coming with her mother's aid in the first fresh days of her baby's life, was showing to Frances two ways to grow to her true spiritual stature: the way of suffering, justly merited; and the way of grace, in which one recieves forgiveness and acceptance as freely as he gives it.

These two ways of growth formed a consistent theme in decades of readings that Cayce gave to hundreds of people. With or without the framework of reincarnation, it made sense to many who took the trouble to study what Cayce said, rather than stopping at the marvel at his psychic feats.

Five months later came another dream that related to Frances' basic value system. Like many dreams which came to those who were seriously studying their dreams with him, Cayce said that this was a "lesson" dream, meant to help Frances put her life journey in perspective. It was a dream of a close friend of hers who had recently died, in which his actual expiring was symbolically re-enacted.

Regarding my mother and her pointing out a crowd to me; about David, who lay dying. He was in the last stage of the process. I saw his eyes glazed. My mother seemed to call attention to this. Then in a final effort, he tried to get up. Those about him would not permit. My mother showed me that of course they would not. Then he dropped back and died. I cried, at which my mother instructed me not to cry.

The dream was about David, according to Cayce, because he represented to Frances someone of notable wealth and social position—concerns that Frances was tempted to rate too highly. The dying showed her graphically how death puts everyone at one level—and no last-minute action can do anything about it. David's effort to get up was a dramatization of the importance of will-power—what everyone must use to make life an unfolding, rather than a long indulgence which fails at last to yield the understanding and peace that should be there—from "the life well-lived and in service to others."

This dream preview of the exact events of dying was meant, as Cayce saw it, to give Frances more than arcane knowledge of life beyond the grave. It was meant to put her daily living into proper perspective, so that she might choose her proper working values. Such values were not a matter, he emphasized, of putting on a long face. Nor should Frances be always thinking of death and the future. Life was to be lived now.

"Yet it is not all of life to live, nor all of death to die," he continued. Living or dying, the soul must account to itself for all it has thought and done. For it is in the nature of the soul to return to the "Whole" which created it, yet to reserve in itself the power to know itself an individual, and all it has been and done.

Nobody escapes himself. What kind of Frances did Frances want to journey with, through time and death?

As though to emphasize that real values were known in the little things of life, a dream which came soon after was one which Cayce described as presented through the efforts of the mother, though she did not appear in it. Frances reported:

Saw the baby real sick—stomach upset and vomiting.

Seemed I should give it Milk of Magnesia.

The dream showed, as Cayce often said of health dreams, only the extremity of what could happen, if the baby's present need were neglected. The remedy of the dream, he said, was exactly right to counteract the baby's acidity, and should be taken at once—with his diet watched more carefully in the future.

Even more prosaic was a little dream fragment which Aaron reported to Cayce for Frances. *"Her mother told her that Frances was buying an evening dress."* Here Frances could see, said Cayce, that her mother was as completely aware of her daughter's "secular affairs" as of her "spiritual affairs." She was finding her daughter's whole life, including her social life "the same and as interesting as in physical life."

The underlying character of the mother's relation to her daughter was the theme of a dream that came a month later. This dream needed no interpretation by Cayce. It began with a reference to a sick relative.

Said my mother: "Your sister-in-law will be all right. We are all working for her recovery here." Then said someone else, or my mother, "Yes, that is the trouble. We cannot do what we want to do—go on and develop, because we still have dear ones on earth that need our help. This keeps us close to earth. We have to always be looking after you young people."

Later my mother showed me this latter in emblematical fashion, showing me how the mother love I have for my baby survives in the spiritual individuality of a cosmic entity, as for example it does in her for me. Thus she gave me another lesson of the life after death, and of all life, love and close relationship of loved ones—of life's greater joy and glory depending upon service. It was as follows: I was preparing to go home to Mississippi, where I wanted to go. I was saying good-bye to all and my mother was packing my trunk. Seeing my baby, I changed my mind about going, and stayed with my baby.

Just so, my mother, loving me, her baby, stays close to earth with me, although the freedom of the universe holds an alluring invitation for the application of her present spirit power. Correct?

It was true, Cayce said, that her mother was "in physical plane or earth's sphere as yet, until that force leads on in its ever-developing, toward that oneness with the All-Force, see?" The time would come when the mother would move on, along her own soul's path of growth. For the present, Frances could count on her steady help, as was apparent in one of the last dreams Frances sent to Cayce for interpretation.

I saw my mother very distinctly. I was sending her a telegram that she was going to die.

This was no dream of warning or foreboding, according to Cayce. On the contrary, it showed Frances in a conscious act of acceptance of her mother's state. It signaled Frances' own deep awareness that her mother would give her all the guidance and protection she needed for her own life or for her baby, if she would rely from now on upon her own intuition and upon her mother's influence. Not even death could now take her by surprise.

When Frances next asked Cayce's counsel about proper care for the baby while she went on a six-weeks' trip, he gave her none. When she had such definite assurance of her mother's aid, he asked, and so many experiences of learning to work with her mother, why did she need Cayce?

Frances had found her way through the country of death.

She had found the thread of love that stretches from life beyond the grave.

Now she must weave her life of it.

Frances had her own view of the adventure on which her dreams had led her for four years. When the Cayce Hospital was at last completed at Virginia Beach, she mounted the speaker's platform on that windy Armistice Day of 1929, and shyly took her turn among the others who brought greetings. Her words were proper and formal, but they carried her thought:

> *May this institution so spread its teachings as to help and give guidance and understanding to all peoples of all lands—as the teachings have aided me to gain an understanding of the oneness of life and force.*

PART II. HOW TO WORK WITH DREAMS

CHAPTER V. CAYCE'S SKILL—AND THE DREAMER'S

Through the forty years in which Edgar Cayce exercised his puzzling gift, he often found his readings presenting as fact something his listeners considered unlikely.

The Cayce readings recommended osteopathy alongside of respectable drugs and surgery, when osteopathy was classified solely as quack medicine. They traced psychosomatic elements in illness—in perhaps a quarter of his readings—when only Viennese specialists considered psychogenic causes important. They described certain vitamins before these were isolated in the laboratory. They specified endocrine gland functions only discovered after Cayce's death.

In the 1930's, two decades before the discovery of the Dead Sea Scrolls at Qumran, the Cayce readings explained how ancient Essene and other centers of Covenanters were run, at the Dead Sea and elsewhere. In the 1940's, when France was occupied and faced a forlorn future, they predicted its post-war return as an independent European power. In the 1920's, long before the United Nations was founded, they insisted that the League of Nations had been the right proposal for mankind's outlawing of war.

Decades before Zen Buddhism and Hindu meditation were discussed on American campuses, they specified the procedures of deep meditation, and recommended it for everyone. They described earthquakes before they occurred, and noted the fault-lines involved. They produced a dissertation on the camber of airplane wings, a decade ahead of aeronautical research. They predicted the basic life patterns of newborn babies—and it required a generation to verify how incredibly accurate they were.

Those who studied the Cayce readings were staggered at

the seeming range of their vision, which moved freely from microorganisms to life after death, from Persian history to stock market prices, from buried oil fields to buried musical genius in a child.

They also noted that the Cayce readings did not function as a psychic microscope or telescope. The readings were methodically engaged in building people, all through the forty years of his activity as the best-known psychic of modern times.

Edgar Cayce in trance presented every finding in terms of the difference it could make in someone's life. He refused to tell people whatever they could not constructively use. He would not give one person an unfair advantage over others. He turned every quest for aid into a quest for meaning, as well. When people turned to him for medical counsel, he asked them, one way or another, "What will you do with your life if you recover?" He was evidently much more than a psychic oddity. He was a coach, an analyst, a teacher, a spiritual director, to those who sought his aid.

His total gift—both for information and for penetrating counsel on individual values—served to make his strangest claim of all seem this one: "I don't do anything you can't do."

He said it over and over again to visitors, the famed and the nobodies, who came to talk with him wherever he lived. He said it wide awake, smiling but nonetheless seriously. And he said it in trance, again and again, explaining the processes at work.

He insisted that what people saw in Edgar Cayce was not unique in principle, though it might be striking. They were seeing the operation of laws, quite natural laws. They were seeing laws which they themselves could learn to use.

To be sure, not everyone who learned to understand and apply the laws would come out precisely where Cayce did. Some would have notably different gifts—for example, intellectual scholarship or administrative leadership—in which their psychic abilities and inward spirituality would help them as he was helped. Not everyone would have the same degree of gifts: there were geniuses in every field. Some—he said—would be better psychics than he: he was emphatic about the claim, and told one man he could learn to give a certain kind of readings awake, while he told another that he could learn (through a lifetime of disciplined work) even to raise the dead—capacities he said were far beyond Edgar Cayce in this lifetime.

The claim that anyone could do, in some measure, what Edgar Cayce did, may well have been the boldest claim he ever made.

But he did not let the claim hang in the air. He gave people a laboratory where they could investigate the claim for themselves. He urged them to recall and study their dreams. In dreams, he said, people could experience for themselves every important kind of psychic phenomenon, and every level of helpful psychological and religious counsel. What is more, they could, through dreams, learn the laws of these things and undergo a spontaneous and tailored dream-training program in the use of the laws—provided that in their waking life they put to constructive use everything they learned in the dreams.

It was an extraordinary claim for dreams.

When Cayce died, he left behind four complete cases of individuals whom he had trained, through the study of hundreds of their dreams by means of his readings, to broaden and deepen their natural gifts—psychic gifts, intellectual gifts, financial gifts, leadership gifts, artistic gifts, healing gifts, gifts of loving, gifts of wisdom, gifts of training others.

One of these cases was his own, a record of 106 dreams interpreted in sixty-nine readings, given in the years 1924 to 1940. He undertook the study of his own dreams because, shortly after he moved to Virginia Beach, he was told to do so by his own readings. Many who might not accept what he seemed to do in trance, he was told, would be willing to experiment with their own dreams, if he set them an example. In the systematic recording and study of their dreams there could unfold "much that may be worthwhile to the minds of many individuals, who will hearken and apply the same lessons and truths, as gained from same [study], to their individual lives."

The reading added a pregnant comment, indicating—as was always the emphasis over the years—that the right way to approach people about what Edgar Cayce did was *not* to try to sell them on Cayce's phenomena. Instead, others should be equipped with laws or "truths" which they could try out for themselves. It was not Cayce who mattered. "Not necessary to believe in the works of Edgar Cayce," the reading said bluntly. What was needful was for others to try out for themselves the "truths as manifested through same, see?" Dreams, it said, were an excellent way to do it.

The same reading drew a close parallel between Edgar Cayce's trance state and what occurs in sleep. "At the present," the reading began, describing his trance, "we find body and mind in that passive state, wherein the action of positive suggestion from physical mind"—this meant Cayce's own prayerful suggestion that put him in trance, reinforced by hypnotic suggestion from his wife—"directs toward the Universal Forces, as found in subconscious direction." It was the same process described for dreamers before, where their own subconscious could in dreams approach the Universal Forces, through superconscious tuning processes. This was all Edgar Cayce did in readings, except that he was also "capable of using physical faculties" to speak, and was simultaneously using resources which dreamers might approach singly or occasionally: "the cosmic and spiritual and superconscious forces all in action" at once.

Driving home its point about dream study, the reading went on, "Dreams, then, that come to the entity [Edgar Cayce] may be the correlation of any or all of these faculties, and should be made record of," if Cayce were to show people how their nighttime states reproduced his trance state.

Achieving a sleep state precisely like Edgar Cayce's trance became a reality to Frances—another one of the four dreamers he trained. She herself experienced in dreams not only telepathy, visions of the future, medical counsel, and insight into both relatives and strangers, but glimpses of stock movements and of life beyond death. Still, she found it hard to believe that she was using variations of the same process as Edgar Cayce used.

Then one afternoon during a nap, after she had been working on her dreams for two years, she had the following memorable experience:

About 3:00 PM, just after getting to sleep, talking direct to myself (not seeing myself talking, but myself doing the talking, but aware of myself doing it), saying: "Now my body is assuming its normal forces, and will be able and will give such information as is desired of it at the present time. The physical body will be perfectly normal and will give that information now."

She was paraphrasing instructions she had heard given to Edgar Cayce as the prologue to each reading-period, shortly after his regular breathing indicated he was in deep trance. Frances continued by recording her thoughts at the time of her experience.

"Now I am in the same condition that Cayce is in when he gives a reading. Only my heart is beating, and higher organs functioning (otherwise the body is still). Wouldn't my husband or the maid think it queer to hear me talking while in this condition? What would they think if they came in and heard me now?"

After a bit she found herself repeating the suggestion she had heard Mrs. Cayce employ, to bring her husband out of trance.

"Now my physical forces" . . . etc., etc. (right through the entire procedure of awakening, word for word as in a reading), until "Now perfectly normal and perfectly balanced, I will wake up." Then I did wake up. I jumped up, a little frightened and quite dizzy. I had a peculiar sensation at the back of my head. I felt hungry and after eating a little the dizziness passed away. The experience lasted about 25 minutes. Thereafter I went to sleep again, to sleep for quite a while—normally.

Frances asked, when she wrote to Cayce, "Was I in the same condition Cayce is in while giving a reading?" The answer from the sleeping Cayce was unequivocal: "The same."

When she asked how she had given herself the suggestion, when Cayce typically needed it given to him, she was told that her mother had helped her, from the next plane, though she had not realized it in the dream.

The experience had come to her, Cayce reported, for several reasons. She had been trying to grasp the nature of consciousness after death. So this dream experience had put her into a deathlike state, yet allowed her to keep in touch with her body. Further, she had sought to understand what Cayce did, and the dream came to help her do so, for "with the experience there comes the more reality" by understanding laws and processes at work; "in experience is the knowledge of conditions and the surrounding elements obtained."

Finally, the dream had occurred to show her one direction for her service to others, if she chose, and if she prepared herself correctly. Of course, Frances asked how she might do it again, taking up someone's physical disease, as she had seen Cayce do.

He cautioned her to move slowly, studying every such experience that happened to her, until she thoroughly grasped the processes at work. If she did this studying, and kept her waking life one of prayerful, loving service to others, she could then expect a series of such dream experiences—a kind of inward training program.

But she would have to face a most important question in seeking such development. Why was she doing it? If she sought it for fame or for power over others, or as compensation for failures or guilts in her life, she would get nowhere.

This warning, which Cayce repeated to everyone who sought serious psychic development, may have frightened Frances. Or she may have simply been distracted by the outward events in her life, which in two or three years pressed her hard. At any rate, she did not report achieving this state again—except in the modified form in which she sought attunement with her mother for guidance on her baby.

But she knew why Cayce claimed, over and over again, that anybody could do what he did—and could start doing it in dreams.

Dreams and Medical Readings

Edgar Caycc first received national attention in 1910, when a physician reported on him to a medical society, meeting in Boston. By then he had given medical counsel to doctors for several years.

Medical aid was the form in which his hypnotic abilities had first appeared, when a physician in his home town asked him to diagnose and prescribe for patients—as a few European hypnotic subjects had reportedly done.

The whole idea had seemed ridiculous to the young Edgar Cayce. He had no education beyond grade school, and his vocational experience was clerking in bookstores and assisting a photographer. Yet when unconscious he showed the capacity to go over a human body like a mental x-ray, using medical terms he had never heard, and then to prescribe complex medical treatments or refer patients to specialists.

The phenomenon of the "psychic diagnostician," as the newspapers called him, began as a novelty, a sort of natural wonder like a waterfall. But by the middle of Cayce's life his gift had become stable and respected enough to generate the "Cayce Hospital" at Virginia Beach, with a complete medical staff, and a university with a full faculty, administration, student body and football teams—Atlantic University at Virginia Beach, which operated until the Depression closed it.

Of the thirteen thousand or more readings recorded and kept in Cayce's lifetime (and thousands went unrecorded before he moved to Dayton, Ohio, in 1923), more than two-thirds were devoted to medical counsel for individuals, on a range of ailments that would equal the variety in a sizeable clinic.

Why was so much of his psychic effort medical? His own readings said it was because one of his best past lifetimes had found him as a dedicated healer, in ancient Persia, and that this inclination to aid people in pain had continued as part of his heritage as a soul. There was also the effect of his memorable prayer and vision as a boy of twelve, when he had asked, while studying the Bible, to be of service to his fellow man as had Biblical figures, and "especially to children." Perhaps there were other contributing elements.

Cayce held high the figure of Jesus, whose ministry included healing. And in pragmatic American culture, a psychic would receive no hearing without a "useful" gift.

A typical medical reading, which Cayce called a "physical reading" rather than "medical" (out of determination that those he helped should work with their doctors, not using him in their stead), began by estimating the seriousness of the ailment that brought the person to him. Then the reading moved to the critical point of malfunction in the body—whether an infection or an injury or some other abnormality. Sometimes this point was different from what the patient or his doctor might expect—as Cayce located the critical point in epilepsy in the abdomen, and only secondarily in the brain. He would trace the fundamental pathology of the body he was looking at, as calmly as though he were studying a battery of x-rays and laboratory reports, instead of lying unconscious on a couch, often hundreds of miles from a patient he had never seen.

Usually he would next move through the major systems of the body, noting the history of each in the particular patient, as well as its present function—and even the precise symptoms and how they felt to the patient at particular times of day or night. He made a special point of noting how each system contributed to the malfunction or distortion of another system, and often insisted that the whole person had to be treated—not just a given disease-entity with a convenient medical name.

First came the circulatory systems, both blood and lymphatic. He seemed to be able to supply blood count statistics without difficulty, as well as toxins in the blood stream, blood presssure, and sources of infection, or constriction in the circulation. He examined endocrine function as it appeared in the blood, blood sugar, and microorganisms (he could even describe how one would look under magnification).

Then he went on to the nervous systems, cerebrospinal, and autonomic, describing impairment or irregularities. If any of the senses functioned abnormally, he might describe how and why, noting also reaction times, pain patterns, over-stimulation or under-stimulation to parts of the body.

He singled out particular nerves and ganglia, where necessary, tracing their exact location and function in the body.

Next came the major organ systems of the body. He looked at the condition of the brain. Then he went on to the respiratory system, from nose to lungs, noting typical congestion patterns, history of TB, and—when necessary—what x-rays would show. Next came the heart and its pulmonary system for oxygenating the blood; he found no difficulty in indicating pulse, heart valve operation, deposits in or around the heart, and history of heart disease. Then it was time to examine the entire digestive system, from mouth to excretory organs. He often commented on acid-alkaline balance, on peristalsis, on the secretions of liver and pancreas, on eliminations and kidney function. Sexual and childbearing organ systems were examined when appropriate, and throughout special attention was given to endocrine function—with the attendant questions of metabolism and of the body's patterns in growth and healing.

By this point in a reading, Cayce had been speaking in an unconscious state for over half an hour. It was time for him to move to the complicated question of treatment. He did it with equal thoroughness, for he insisted on mapping out a program to rebuild the patient and remove the cause of the ailment, not simply relieve symptoms.

He did not hesitate to prescribe sophisticated drugs, even narcotics, so long as these were given under a physician's supervision. Not infrequently he spelled out a compound in detailed grams and minims, for a pharmacist to follow. But he also singled out commercial products and used them by name—unless the manufacturer changed their formulas, which he promptly noted and corrected by suggesting a pharmacist's additions. Nor did he hesitate to recommend surgery, where he thought it was necessary, even when physicians were advising against it: He was quite capable of specifying the exact incision, procedure, and drainage.

But there was a heavier weight given to all types of physiotherapy, in his medical counsel, than one would find in the prescriptions and care of the typical family doctor. Behind this weight lay his insistence that the body should be helped to cure itself, as far as possible, and protected from the blows of needless chemicals or knife, which might accomplish a cure but weaken the system. So his readings contained baths, packs, colonics, exercises, manipulative therapy, electrotherapy, sweats, massages and oils.

They were also detailed in prescription of diet—both special diets and regular daily diets, as well as food supplements and tonics. His diets were not faddist, but comprised a part of his medical readings which early won wide recognition for their soundness. Handling food, he sometimes insisted, as he did with medication, that there were specific body cycles to be followed—a feature of medicine not as yet widely practiced, perhaps because the instrumentation to determine these cycles is not always available at the level of accuracy that the sleeping Cayce demonstrated.

Changes in attitude, habits, outlooks, recreation, life style and vocation, as well as religious orientation, came under discussion in his therapy—sometimes at the head of the list of treatments. Hypnosis and psychotherapy were at times recommended, as well as group therapy and even intercessory prayer by others. But most often the patient himself was told to rebuild his own inner life by examining its foundations and its impact on those around him, as well as on his health.

Perhaps the most striking feature in the medical readings was not the sleeping Cayce's diagnostic work; one could at least imagine him going out to look over a patient with x-ray vision (although in point of fact he claimed that the diagnosis came from the patient's own subconscious, which knew the body better than Cayce did). And it was not his encyclopedic knowledge of medical terms and a staggering variety of treatments; one could at least imagine a mind of superb memory, augmented by unseen medical counsel. What shocked observers as much as any feature of these readings was his seeming access to a complete directory of medical aids. He could instantly specify the best surgeon for treating a particular condition, and where he was located. He could specify where to order an unknown drug. He could identify where climate and altitude would be best for the patient—and even mention the local golf courses. Hearing this facility at work, and knowing of its accuracy in hundreds of readings, the listener was often driven to postulate some sort of a "universal consciousness," such as that which Cayce himself said he was tapping.

Yet Cayce insisted that all he did in his medical readings was capable of duplication in dreams—if the dreamer needed it and could understand it. At the very least, the dreamer who sought it would find himself directed where to get help, when, and why, for himself and his loved ones.

To be sure, those who had a natural bent towards medicine, as did Frances, would find more of such dream material than others whose major focus might be on art or history. But the body would make its needs known in dreams, and even suggest therapy.

Frances' husband, Aaron, dreamed of manipulative therapy for his ailing mother:

> *I said to my mother, "Now I am going to give you this osteopath treatment myself." I gave it more as Dr. H. (of Virginia) does, kneading and spreading cervicals gently, rather than roughly cracking them.*

In his dream he was seeing exactly the care needed by his mother, Cayce reported, only it should be given by a doctor and not by the dreamer. To make things easier, Cayce then named a doctor in New York who would do it properly: "Marshall would be well with this, Dan Marshall." Since Aaron had never heard of him (very likely Cayce awake had never heard of him), he asked, "Will you give the address?" Cayce's reply was notable: "New York. Look in the telephone book—put self to some trouble."

Cayce's unending problem in training dreamers was to get them to rely on themselves, asleep or awake. He did not seek little Cayce-ites. He wanted capable, self-reliant people, using the talents with which they were endowed, and learning new laws to apply.

As a good coach, he had to keep encouraging his dreamers. He used all his medical skill to do it.

When women dreamed of pregnancy, he added the exact dates within which they should conceive. Then he challenged them to dream the sex of the baby, which he could confirm. It was up to them to learn to dream helpfully. If they dreamed the baby's formula was wrong, he corrected it, but pressed them to try for further leads to check with him.

When a man dreamed that his riding breeches were too large, Cayce was delighted with his progress in dreaming of medical care. The dream was noting, he said, that riding was good for the dreamer, but not too much of it. When another dreamer heard himself warned not to go to football games he loved, Cayce reinforced the warning, and asked the man to dream why the warning had come. He did. It was because of the danger of ear infection. Cayce agreed, and spelled out the treatment to free the dreamer to go to the games. And in a burst of encouragement he even told the dreamer which games his alma mater would win in the rest of the season—providing the starting lineup was not changed.

Dreams and Psychological Readings

Edgar Cayce was forty-five years old and had been using his gift for two decades when there first appeared the type of reading which was to become the second most numerous in his files: the psychological readings, which he called "life readings." There were, when he died, approximately twenty-five hundred of these, given for people of all ages and walks of life, beginning with his own family and relatives. The contents of these readings, too, he claimed, could be paralleled in dreams.

Similar in many ways to the medical readings, they examined the systems of the psyche instead of systems of the body.

At the very start of these readings the sleeping Cayce often spoke in a half-voice, as though to himself, while examining records. Going back year by year in the individual's life, he noted out loud the telling developments, the turning points, the traumas or stresses that had shaped the life—from one or two to a half-dozen items. Then he plunged into assessing an entire personality.

As in the medical readings, he began with a few sweeping comments to characterize what he was dealing with—the person's amplitude of spirit, the relative talents and potential for service, the kind of lessons most needed in the lifetime, the choices that must be made.

Then he began his systematic analysis of the person. First came the individual's temperament, talents, and tendencies of life style (how far outgoing, or an extremist, or reflective, etc.). He took up these questions, which he treated as the innate wiring and plumbing of the personality, however used or misused or ignored by the individual, in a novel fashion. Turning back to a sevenfold framework used by the ancient Greek Stoics, he employed the names of Olympian gods and goddesses, as emblems of trends in the personality. These same structures could, he said, also be correlated with traditions about planets in the Zodiac—though not in a mechanical way. In point of fact, he said, the seven emblems were ways of talking about tendencies of the person which he had developed and refined in interim periods *between* earth lives (a notion which the Stoics also shared).

In so approaching a personality, Cayce used his seven spotlights carefully to highlight trends in the personality. He dealt not only with the strength of individual endowments—for example, intellectual acumen, which he ascribed to "Mercury"—but with the way in which one endowment blended with another— as how "Mercury" might be affected by aggressiveness and force, which he called "Mars."

But in using this framework, Cayce set himself outside the terminology of modern psychology, which nowhere employs a similar typology—not even in the three panels of temperament types used by Sheldon, nor in the eight "functions and attitudes of consciousness" used by Carl Jung.

Sometimes Cayce only briefly discussed these innate structure patterns of the personality, because the individual, he said, was using his will to "set them all at naught." Other times he expanded on them at considerable length, linking them with the person's vocation, personality weaknesses, friendships, artistry, morality, philosophical interests, habits, and leadership capacities. These were the conduits down which the person's natural energy tended to flow, whatever the ends he sought. Often, he said, they were dramatized in abstract dreams, or dreams of structures and designs.

But then Cayce turned to the more dynamic side of personality—the goals and answers toward which the individual was moving, and the powerful drives and fascinations that were taking him there. These were elements which he said came from previous earth lives; they usually appeared, he noted, in dreams of strong sensory and emotional tone.

Cayce's method of taking up earth lives was a simple one. He selected from among the many he said he could see those which he felt were currently relevant for the individual. He warned that other past lives might have had their bearing at some previous point in the present biography, and passed on, while still other lives might come later into focus.

In Cayce's view one is, in some sense, living all his "lives" at the present. A past existence is not left behind like a closed book. It survives into the present much as psychoanalysis says childhood survives into adult life, coloring it in many ways. Cayce saw the full personalities developed in past lives as substructures of the present psyche, coloring all of life after adolescence, and constellated with different lives to the fore, depending on the individual's present behavior.

He insisted that dreams may recall actual scenes and memories from past lives, and that one is likely to dream of the personality drives and problems left as deposits by those lives.

In his "life readings" he sketched, as a rule, from four to six past lives bearing on the present. (When asked, he was able to go back and devote one or more entire reading to a particular life.) He frequently touched on the family and social standing of the individual in each past life as well as on his upbringing, education and talents. He caught the sense of whether the life had reached for clear goals or simply drifted. He singled out talents that might carry over to the present. He tried to convey the sense of belonging, what the main relationships were like and how they unfolded. He set the individual in the framework of the causes, institutions, and movements of his times—especially those that had struck deep chords in the person at that time. He spelled out the individual's name in an English transliteration from whatever language was appropriate—whether Hebrew, Chinese, Sanskrit, Egyptian, American Indian, or some other. And he summarized each life by tersely indicating how far "the entity gained" or "the entity lost."

He gave special attention to that lifetime in which he felt the individual had reached his highest spiritual development, his clearest ideal and greatest service to his fellowman. Often he told people they were already dreaming of this lifetime, in repeated fragments of which he reminded them, and he claimed that one of the main functions of dreaming of past lives was to quicken again the spiritual core of the person.

At the end of the reading, he came into the present, to summarize "the abilities of the entity, that to which it may attain, and how." Here he took up questions of vocation, education, marriage, public service, to suggest how the individual's heritage might be fitted into contemporary culture and into the web of his personal ties. He indicated where the person would find his greatest happiness, do the most good, feel the most alive, keep freshly growing. And he closed his analysis by putting the question of spiritual priorities to the fore: Where did the individual, in his heart, stand with his God?

Frequently there were also questions about practical matters, which Cayce took up one at a time: how to get along with certain relatives, how to decide between job offers, why certain failures kept daunting the person, how to begin a more disciplined life.

It was Cayce's claim, in the hundreds of dream readings he gave, that all of the important matters in his life readings were capable of investigation in the individual's dreams.

It would be no great surprise to a psychoanalyst, or to a modern student of dreams in sleep laboratories, to hear that dreams deal with all the *questions* about temperament, talents, style, drives, goals, commitments, and relationships which Cayce touched upon in his life readings. But it would be outrageous, in the views of most dream students, to expect dreams to present the same *structures* that Cayce described: past lives, and patterns from "interim" experiences. Yet Cayce insisted that dreams, carefully studied, would be found to present both the present questions and the relevant past structures.

He used all of his life-reading skill in coaching dreamers.

When a financier dreamed of himself as a philosopher receiving a degree in academic robes, Cayce told him that he had the talent, from Egyptian and Chinese lives, and encouraged him to proceed. Within four years the man had published a meaty book on life after death, was lecturing monthly at a university, and received the honors he dreamed about.

When a sensitive and verbal young man dreamed of himself in the outfit of an ancient warrior, sword in hand, Cayce confirmed the dreamer's guess that he was glimpsing a past life. But Cayce also challenged the dreamer to discover, through dreams and self-study, how the warrior-self fitted into his present personality. The young man responded, in time, that he was now to use the old fierceness to keep him patient and dogged in serving others, rather than destroying them with his tongue and rebuffs. Cayce agreed, and insisted that the substructure of the warrior in his makeup would help him to develop controlled strength—as something surely did, in the years that followed.

An attractive, ambitious, power-driven woman, an executive in a New York business firm, dreamed of a man to whom she was drawn. He was in her apartment, where she could either seduce him or help him on a creative project in which he was engaged. Cayce suggested that the man in question had once been her son, at a time when she was genuinely self-sacrificing, though strong. By working with him now she could bring out her best side, rather than her predatory instincts.

When a stockbroker began to dream of stocks symbolically in number patterns that indicated their rise and fall, strengths and weaknesses, and even dates and quantities of purchase and sale, Cayce told the dreamer the name of a stranger whom he should consult on the symbology of numbers, and make into a good friend as well—for they had been associated in lifetimes before.

When a banker asked about the strange languages which others told him he spoke in his sleep, Cayce identified these as Egyptian and Celtic, which he indicated could be verified. In addition, he urged the dreamer to notice again the stone tablets which frequently appeared in his sleep (and which the dreamer had not mentioned to Cayce). He could learn to read these Egyptian tablets, Cayce said: "Study to read these up and down, not across."

Cayce told a woman that she could recall in her dreams a past life experience of being brought home from the Crusades as the Moorish wife of a Christian, and could write memorable stories on the conflicts and growth she had known.

In scores of dream readings he showed the dreamer how past life experience had precipitated a present pattern: the way a husband looked down on his wife as a child, the tendency of a dreamer who had once banished others to flee into self-imposed exile when things went wrong with him, the deafness now afflicting a man who too often had turned a "deaf ear" to the cries of others, the reason that classmates kept electing a student to leadership posts. Cayce took what he felt was an authentic bit of "life reading" in the dream, and added his own information and encouragement.

Whether Cayce's claims about reincarnation will ever be verified, by study of age-regression hypnosis, of claimed memories by the living, of dreams, of visions under drugs, and of structures of the psyche, remains problematic. Certainly if they are ever given stature by research, they may add weight of Freud's claim of sexuality in infants, to Rank's studies of the birth trauma, and to Jung's speculations on individual inheritances from a transpersonal or "collective" unconscious.

Dreams and Religious Readings

By the end of his life, Cayce had narrowed the variety of readings he gave to three kinds which together could give a profile of the individual. The "physical reading" could size up a person medically. The "life reading" could size him up psychologically. And what Cayce called a "mental and spiritual reading" could size him up in his relation to the divine.

There were fewer "mental and spiritual" readings than either physical or life readings, partly because they were not so immediately vital as the physical readings, nor as exotic as the life readings. Yet Edgar Cayce took particular joy in giving these straightforward little readings, because they touched on the questions that he felt mattered most in life.

These readings were an analysis of the composition of the whole "entity," the soul in its long journey, somewhat as the other readings had analyzed body and psyche.

To orient the individual receiving the reading, Cayce usually began by a review of what a soul was, and how it functioned in a human body in an earth life. All souls had been created in the beginning at the same time, he insisted and had been given free will to go out into creation, to adventure and experiment. Their destiny was to return to the divine by an informed and conscious act of will, entering into full partnership with the divine in aiding and advancing creation. However, it was their special contribution to the divine that they would remember all they had done and been, enriching the very Godhead itself.

Some of the souls, Cayce reported as calmly as he might report on the American Revolution in an episode of a life reading, had gone to the earth, to "be fruitful, multiply, and subdue it"—indeed to bring to earth's creation the possibility of consciously knowing its relation with the divine from which it had sprung. But these souls had attuned themselves so sharply to affairs of earth that they had become mired in its laws and processes—all elements good of themselves, but a different set of processes than were meant to guide the souls. The souls had lost their native attunement to the divine, and had to be given a way of growing back towards the divine, while experiencing the mysteries of creation and the Creator in the earth that they had chosen. The process of reincarnation was the result.

As each soul moved through life after life, and its interim experiences, it was to perfect its attunement to the divine, and its loving service to its fellows. The mental and spiritual reading was an examination of those two processes in the individual under question.

First was the matter of where the individual constantly turned his thoughts, in daily life. Cayce never tired of insisting that "mind is the builder," capable of bringing the soul into better and more productive relation with the divine lines of force, or taking the soul farther and farther away into its own dead ends.

Dreams, too, in Cayce's view, are often occupied with

the question of the dreamer's habitual thoughts.

An inventor who dreamed that someone stole his invention was becoming so distracted with worry that he could no longer invent well. A pregnant woman dreaming of bills was so concerned about expenses that she was harming her health and the baby's, instead of leaving these matters to the husband who could handle them. A businessman was so suspicious of his partners, as his dreams mirrored, that he was alienating them and bringing on the very betrayal he feared. On the other hand, a man who sought to bring out the best in people saw himself in a dream as having a great time fishing with his friends—fishing for "spiritual food," Cayce said. A man praying for a desperately ill relative saw his prayers like a light in her hospital room, depicted in the dream as brighter or dimmer according to his constancy of focus and desire, and glowing with help for her.

Typically the mental and spiritual reading turned next to what the dreamer put forth in his life, through his vocation, his marriage, his friendships, his commitments to groups and institutions. In different ways Cayce would ask the same question: what is your ideal? In the long run there were only two kinds of ideals: self-serving goals, and the service of others. With a firm scalpel, Cayce cut open the individual's handling of fame, of wealth, of power, of wisdom, of love. He selected whatever was good in the person that could be built upon—motherhood, feeling for the underdog, courage under fire, capacity to take a long view, loyalty to friends—the best of the person's ideals. Then he compared the rest of the person's behavior and challenged him to bring them all into line. Ultimately, Cayce said, the one complete ideal for the human family, though many others were admirable, was the soul who had come to be known as Christ. He often asked the person before him to compare his life with that Life; despite the reality and usefulness of knowing about past lives, this was the Life that counted.

In Cayce's understanding of dreams, a comparison of the dreamer's life with his ideal was occurring in dreams almost every night, however symbolically portrayed, or however small the action examined.

A dreamer who recalled that the night before he was putting on peculiar shoes and shoestrings was told that he had been reminded to keep his feet on the upward path. A man who saw a wet street and streetlights being cleaned was told that his own "way" was being cleansed to receive more light, more truth about his life, which he could share with others. A man whose hobby was home movies saw a revolving light in a projector-like box in a darkroom; it was, said Cayce, a representation of "the Light within," and how the dreamer could, despite constrictions and darkness in his life, reach out to aid his fellowman through many channels. A dreamer who felt, in his dream, compassion for the children of shopclerks, who were waiting outside the store, was told that such compassion was the beginning of authentic sublimation of sexual fantasies such as had often crowded his mind about women clerks.

And a dreamer who heard in his dream only his name called aloud three times was told by Cayce that he had the same experience as the child Samuel in the temple. He should answer with the simple but whole-hearted response, "Use me!"

Whatever counsel or challenge Cayce might offer in his mental and spiritual readings was more than equaled, he felt, in dreams.

Dreams and Business Readings

Right alongside his readings about an individual's relations with the divine, Edgar Cayce gave readings about an individual's relations with his dollars. As he told a man who dreamed of great wealth, money, like learning or skill, "is made to serve its intent and purpose" in the scheme of things if kept in perspective.

Indeed, counsel on business matters was not infrequent in his medical readings and life readings, where vocation, employment and investment directly affected an individual's health and peace of mind. In his view, the divine was not only interested in man's religiousness, or moral propriety. As God could properly be called "the Creative Forces," so He could properly be described as interested in all levels of human creativity: making music, making love, making civilizations, making prayers, making medicines, making homes, and making money.

However, there was always human greed, which tended

to appear when people saw that Cayce could deliver valuable information with his psychic gifts. On this question Cayce was firm. He considered his gift as rightly used for building people, not building fortunes. When it was appropriate to help someone build his income as part of his total growth, Cayce would give financial counsel as readily as he prescribed medicines. However, his stress was always upon what the individual could do for himself. When men of means came to him, as they often did, he questioned them as to what else they wanted to do with their lives besides grow rich; only as they showed a willingness to serve others with their means was he likely to give them sustained financial counsel.

When his own son and two relatives came to him for aid in locating a buried treasure, he told them they were on the right track, and proved it with details of the location and initial finds. But he insisted, in his readings, that they were not prepared for the notoriety and self-esteem which such a find would bring them, and he refused to give them further aid except as their own subconscious might give it to them in dreams—which he would then confirm.

The same values applied in all his business readings. When a dream showed how a group of financiers had taken steps to manipulate the market, he helped the dreamer to respond correctly to the manipulation. But he would give the dreamer no aid when the manipulators were only *contemplating* certain steps; at that point, he said, the men's thoughts remained their own property.

Relatively few sought business readings, and got them, because relatively few seemed to meet Cayce's qualifications. However, several dozen people did seek and receive such aid. And a few individuals secured a total of hundreds of readings on business affairs, chiefly as commentary on dreams.

A business reading was usually addressed to a specific problem: a real estate transaction, incorporation of a firm, consideration of specific employees or partners, stock trends, market opportunities, inventions to be developed. After the main problem was treated by Cayce, the individual or group who sought the reading might then ask questions about a variety of other business concerns. However, most of those who knew Cayce well knew also that in business readings they might come under Cayce's searching eye at any time, with their motives and methods of operation questioned or even rebuked. While he did not often expose people in front of others (he once gave a businessman a dressing down in German—a tongue that Cayce did not know but the businessman did—in order to make his point without embarrassing the man before his associates), he had a way of making clear that he knew where things were amiss in the individual's handling of funds, or handling of responsibilities or relationships. This discouraged many from seeking business counsel from him.

Besides, Cayce was insistent that one could discover through dreams all that he needed for business prosperity, if he was in the right vocation and operating with integrity, as well as using his means to help others less fortunate.

Two of the four dreamers whom he trained through the interpretation of hundreds of their dreams became millionaires over a period of four years, by adding their own dream study to their daily work. The other two were not in business nor seeking wealth as ardently as they sought to unfold other talents, though one achieved equal wealth through her husband.

Cayce used all of his psychic skill to coach his business dreamers.

When a woman dreamed of a coming stock rise in a coastal shipping line, he not only confirmed her dream and advised her to buy, but rewarded her with an extra by giving her the exact date, some ninety days off, when the market would prove best for her to sell (he was correct). When a stockbroker kept dreaming of steel stocks, although he was interested in rails and motors, Cayce helped him to see that the dreams were showing steel as the "criterion" of broad market moves for a certain period—and once even charted the movements of steel stock for an entire year ahead. When an investor dreamed he was riding a New York streetcar, which had in it a posted warning that he should not get off at a public building, Cayce not only showed him that this was a warning against New York subway stocks at the time, but how the dream had depicted the reason: Public officials were planning regulations which would cut the profit of the line. When a financier was planning to form a finance company,

Cayce helped him to evaluate the proposed directors through his dreams. When a dreamer came up with a dream of trouble about a check for $150 in his office, Cayce showed him how he was in fact dreaming of two such checks—one that had come in and was improperly recorded, and one that the dreamer's wife ought to pay out, since she owed it. When a tired businessman went on vacation and dreamed that on his return his desk was shoved aside and his secretary installed in his place, he was simply seeing, Cayce remarked, the priority dictation would have on his return.

Over and over Cayce made clear how dreams could be helpful in business, and then added his own insights to encourage the dreamer and keep him growing. A banker dreamed of a stream of secretaries applying for the position he then had open; Cayce helped him identify what qualities he was seeking—and then added that he should hire the third in line. An entrepreneur saw correctly in his dream, Cayce said, how he could distribute and promote a new product for the care of gums—but the dream had also warned him not to use the relative he was considering to do the job.

Whatever factors influenced the business world—the collapse of a bank, orders to a firm from abroad, rumors, combines, labor troubles, government regulations, credit policies, salesmanship, bold decisionmaking, competition—Cayce proved hundreds of times over that he could correctly and instantly grasp them all. But more important, he proved to dreamers that they could grasp these matters as well, with one major difference: their insights were limited to what bore on their own affairs and on those of their associates. They were businessmen, and they got the business counsel they needed. Cayce was a counselor, and he got what his counselees needed.

Those with whom Cayce worked on dreams, to help them in business matters, were not greedy people—or he would not have helped them. But they did face the pressures of relatives and friends to maintain their wealth and the attendant social station; this brought them under severe Cayce scrutiny at times, exactly as it did in their dreams. There was nothing wrong with the making of money, Cayce insisted. Christ himself, he argued in one trenchant reading, could have made an excellent Wall Street broker while remaining wholly true to his Father. What counted was not dollars but motives. What was the soul trying to accomplish with money on its journey through earth lives?

Dreams and Readings on Hidden Resources

Because of his strange ability, Cayce was often approached to locate something hidden or lost. In earlier years he had tried a number of ventures of this sort, but towards the end of his life he was less inclined to get involved. In solving crimes, he had discovered his own psyche was touched and shocked by the violence of the criminal; his own readings told him that using his skill for this purpose was like cutting down trees with a razorblade. He could do it—but why?

When it came to mines and oil wells, he had helped others make fortunes. But he had also seen the investors fall apart as individuals and as a group, overcome with greed and jealousy of one another.

His readings told him that he could himself make legitimate money locating buried treasure, if he could handle his own motives and the consequences of his act. At one of the several times when he tried this, he was off on a journey to help a group of businessmen locate a treasure, with his wife and secretary along. The following dream sent him home:

> *It seemed we were going to take a reading about my grandmother. We knew she was alive again and someone told us to go to a certain place and we would find her. It seemed like a storeroom, or an undertaking establishment. We found my grandmother with vines growing all around and over her. My wife and secretary and I were cutting them away, so there would be no trouble about the reading locating her. Then we started out, talking about how wonderful it would be if this could be proven to people. At the door we met three dogs of different kinds. We tried to get them out, but one got loose and ran back toward*

the dead body. We started running after him, but suddenly I realized it was all a dream and I knew the interpretation of it. It meant that we three were letting our work go to the dogs while we were trying to do something we had no business to do.

While Cayce felt reasonably sure he had the sense of his dream, he submitted it for a reading, anyway. The reading confirmed that the pulling away of vines represented what had engaged him in tramping with the treasure seekers; he was dreaming of the venture, which had for weeks crowded out his medical or vocational aid to others. But more important, it said, the three dogs were himself, his wife, and his secretary, who had started off as pleasant as tail-wagging canines might be, but had developed under the strain dispositions that led to snapping and rending. In this circumstance what good Cayce might do was bound to be spoken poorly of, and he would not gain enough from the treasure nor the feat to be worth the price.

Then the dream commented on the theme of resurrection of the grandmother. His proper concern was with "awakening" people to their true natures and states; that was the purpose of his gift. But he had incorrectly felt that proving he could locate treasure with his gift would accomplish such awakening—certainly nothing of the depth and power of the New Testament resurrection motif with which he had invested the treasure hunt. People had to be awakened individually, with whatever they could use and apply in their own lives, not by the publicity of a psychic stunt.

His readings on the hidden or lost showed similiar reserve when a woman came to him with a dream at the time of the Lindbergh kidnapping. He confirmed every detail in the dream, such as the roles of the nurse and of the gardener. He confirmed the use of a getaway boat on the Potomac, and even corrected her spelling of its name. The town of Arlington which she had somehow located in Germany, in the dream, was instead Arlington, Virginia, but approached by German-speaking principals in the dream. Still, he would not tell her exactly where the baby's body was located. Instead, he urged her to dream again and get the rest of the details, which he would gladly confirm. He even added that if she continued the chase in her dream she would go to Puget Sound. But he would not put her psyche under the stress of more notoriety, from the public solving of the crime, than her own subconscious would do. The next step remained with her and her motives and total strength as a person. She never returned with a further dream.

But she had seen, as did others, that whatever was lost or hidden and could rightfully be discovered by the dreamer, could be disclosed to him in a dream, provided he was ready to handle it. For example, a businessman felt he should invite his overbearing mother to live with him and his young wife. His dream told him emphatically otherwise, but then correctly supplied the address of an apartment building where he could place her not far away. Cayce was delighted to see his pupil making progress in practical use of his dreams.

Dreams and Readings on Social Change

An important body of readings which accumulated in Cayce's files over the years was a file on the progress of a small social movement, bent on changing certain aspects of American life. Its central concern was not civil rights, nor the rights of labor, nor birth control, nor international peace, nor psychoanalysis, nor health foods—though Cayce did give a limited number of readings on all of these matters.

The movement whose growth he coached through his readings, through years of changing personnel and programs and policies, was the activity of a small group of people who felt that Cayce's own work was significant, and representative of concerns that many would share if they understood them. They called this little movement simply "the Work," and readings on "the Work" remain some of the most interesting that Cayce gave.

These readings were astonishingly detached about the personal welfare and fame of Edgar Cayce. Cayce ought to be provided for, the "Work readings" made clear, but the right concern was not Cayce. It was the processes in which individuals could learn to help themselves, could undergo the "awakening" that had been symbolized, for example, in

Cayce's dream of his grandmother. The awakening sought was not to some simple dogma, such as belief in life after death or in psychic phenomena, or in reincarnation. And certainly not to belief in Cayce. Nothing less than that each soul who came to them should awaken to his full creative stature as a son of "the Most High" would suffice as a goal for "the Work." But such awakening required starting where each man was, and building on his particular needs and talents. So they were going to have to deal in medicine, business, philosophy, psychology, physics, social justice, education—in a great many matters. And they were going to have to begin with what they had, right in the Cayce family and his closest associates, while waiting for others with different talents to join them.

Some of Cayce's associates were counseled on where to get an education, some on their vocations, some on their attitudes. As Cayce's life unfolded, the "Work" came to include the founding and operation of the hospital, and the university. When these were closed, the "Work" turned toward the development of spiritual depth and quality in a number of Virginia friends—ordinary people, who brought themselves under discipline and produced a little manual of the devotional life called *A Search for God*.

The history of the Cayce life and work was a microcosm of movements for serious social change. His readings dealt with every aspect of such a movement: its philosophy, its goals, its leadership, its covenants and corporations, its climate of daily work, its stages. Every lasting movement, they insisted, must proceed "first to the individual, then to the group, then to the classes, then to the masses." In this the Cayce sources were adamant, though many sought to promote Cayce by the usual advertising means. Social change had to be accomplished, his readings affirmed, by building and rebuilding one life at a time, supporting it with primary groupings at home and at work and in church and community, and then moving on to develop—over a period of years—exactly this same process with leaders in various professions and walks of life. Only then could something emerge so widespread, so well-understood and practiced, that it would touch masses of people.

In Cayce's view, every aspect of the growth of a social movement could be properly informed and guided by dreams. He used all of his skill to communicate this to the dreamers with whom he worked.

When they dreamed that the hospital could become reality, in times of doubt and difficulty, he showed them how their dreams were prophetic in quality, and not merely wishes. When the question of financing the hospital arrived at its last stages, he helped a dreamer to follow his dreams right to the office where the necessary mortgage could be placed. When the university was to be closed, he helped one dreamer see how the president was going on to new levels of personal and family growth, rather than stopping with present humiliation and defeat. When the study groups began their work, he showed the members how they could counsel each other through their own dreams, and could grow in grace to the point of true visions of Christ, through their dreams—if their lives were being spent for others. He coached dreamers to select board members through dreams, and then to improve attitudes on the board. He helped one dreamer encourage a hospital backer—to stop him from going off the deep end on a project.

The dream readings in the Cayce file showed every step of his "Work" previewed and guided in dreams, from 1924 until his death in 1945. The dreams even included one on Cayce's death, and the consequences for his life's labors—adding the little touch that his wife would die very shortly after him (which proved exactly true). They pointed to the possibility that anyone responsibly concerned in a movement for social change, social service, or social justice, might well seek nightly guidance in his dreams—precisely as had many Biblical figures.

Dreams and Topical Readings

From time to time a group of individuals interested in Cayce's work, or a researcher or writer on a particular topic, would secure one of a small number of readings not devoted to the needs of an individual or group, but to a body of subject matter. Once again, their ability to get the sleeping Cayce to supply such information was determined by what they intended to do with it. If they sought novelty, or recondite information about the soul's journey for their own amazement, or material on an ancient civilization with which to impress others, they might expect little or nothing from the sleeping Cayce, and perhaps a lecture on their own spiritual growth instead. Still, on a number of occasions over the years topical readings were both sought and received.

An international YMCA leader, a man of much faith and good mind, secured information on the authorship of New Testament books—information previously refused to others, who were told that the biblical question for them was whether they could apply it in their own lives. Frances' husband, who was studying life after death, sought and received essays on conditions in the next plane, as well as readings on evolution, and the interplay of heredity and environment. A concerned group of Cayce's associates sought and received topical readings on international affairs, on the nature of Cayce's own gift, on the ancient and much-doubted civilization of Atlantis.

A reading was sought and secured on the causes and cure of the common cold. A small series was secured on the events leading up to and including the birth of Jesus. An entire series of topical readings, supplemented by analyses of how well a study group was understanding them, produced the little manual of spiritual growth, *A Search for God,* as well as a collection of studies of the book of Revelation. Yet another series was given to a group investigating healing by prayer.

Of all the varieties of Cayce readings, the topical reading must have seemed the least likely to be duplicated by dreams. But Cayce showed his dreamers, especially two of the four major subjects that he coached, that dreams were capable of producing extensive verbal essays—complete with diagrams and acted-out illustrations. Indeed, the serious students of their dreams learned to expect that kind of dream which combined a scene with an explanation of it—whether by a voice in their dreams or by a series of coherent thoughts.

Most of the essay dreams, in the Cayce view, originated in efforts of the dreamer's subconscious to teach him something he needed to understand in his daily life and in his studies; often such dreams had the setting of a school. Sometimes essay dreams originated with the dreamer's higher self, and sometimes the major part of the instruction came from a discarnate entity or guide who was helping the dreamer—according to Cayce.

Cayce used all of his skill at securing information to coach dreamers on their dreams of a topical nature.

When a stockbroker dreamed about how the "spirit" of a stock enters into predicting its future movements (and found the essay illustrated by the intentions of people going to a movie), Cayce confirmed the analysis and then showed the dreamer how to distinguish accurate stock leads in dreams from those which were only pictures of stock tendencies. When a Jew dreamed about the question of the work of Christ, Cayce encouraged him on the accuracy of the dream analysis, and added some illustrations of his own. When an American businessman dreamed about the forces breeding revolution in China, Cayce was quick to encourage the dreamer to put his concern into action—especially by studying Chinese affairs to write about them.

Cayce worked on dream-essays on how it feels to die, how the living and the dead communicate, how an individual reaches out to "Universal Forces," what souls can learn from animal creation, what suicide entails, how dreams work, how science and religion fit together, and how moral judgments are made.

In summary, the story of Cayce's forty years of trance counsel is a story of a cornucopia of information, some of it verified and some of it far from verified. It is also the story of the building of human beings, within a clear and cogent scheme of values which did not waver over the years. It is a staggering picture of the unknown potential of the human mind, in touch with some sort of More than itself.

But no claim in the entire Cayce story is more striking than the one he made for decades, right up until the end of his life: that others can do what he did—beginning with their dreams.

CHAPTER VI. GLIMPSES OF THE LAWS OF DREAMING

Edgar Cayce showed his dreamers that the same laws which produced his readings also produced their dreams.

He did not spell out and name these laws, as a scientist might do. Whatever he explained, his readings said, had to be partly filtered through the capacity and terminology of his own psyche, and that of his listeners. Since none were scientists, he gave practical counsel on one dream and one life at a time. But occasionally he offered insights that lit up the landscape of dreaming. And then he urged the dreamers to "study, study, study."

Glimpses of Lawful Patterns in Dreaming

Whatever Cayce's mind was doing when he gave readings, it was not without lawful limits.

He had to be directed to his targets by hypnotic suggestions. For medical counsel he needed the address of the individual who sought aid. For psychological readings he needed the birth date of the individual. And for topical readings, or those on hidden resources, he had to be told both what was sought, and the names and location of those seeking.

Often those who wanted one type of counsel would request, in the question period following the reading, counsel of another kind. When Cayce was especially keyed up, or relating deeply to the person seeking aid, they might get the desired medical information in a business reading, or counsel for a loved one in a dream reading. But more often they would be told, "We do not have this"; and instructed to seek a different type of reading.

Cayce explained to his dreamers that their dream-focus had similar limits. He coached them to set before their minds, by hard study, concentration, and activity, whatever they sought aid upon through dreams. Stock information would come in dreams to one who studied stocks, medical prescriptions to one charged with the health of others, spiritual counsel to one who straightened his paths before his Maker, past life information to one who tried to understand his urges. Dreams were limited by the conscious focus of the dreamer.

Cayce's readings were limited to the information and guidance which an individual could constructively use; it was the same with dreams, said Cayce. There was no point in resolving to dream of international affairs, or of ancient Egyptian times, or of policies of the Federal Reserve system, or of bacteria in a given disease, unless the dreamer were in a position to do something about these. Such information was available through the subconscious and the other resources it would tap, as Cayce felt his own readings showed. But the psyche protected its balance by feeding the dreamer limited material. It operated by laws of self-regulation.

Cayce's readings showed considerable variation in form, from day to day and year to year. As he spoke in trance of these variations, he said the laws at work also affected the form of dreams.

His readings varied in length, as do dreams. The shortest and most abrupt of his dream readings occupied two sentences; it was a reading given on one of his own dreams, which refused to interpret it, telling him he had done nothing about the last dreams interpreted for him. But there were also interpretations of dreams that occupied pages of transcribed notes. Other types of readings showed similar variations in length, from curt answers to long explanations.

His readings varied in clarity of communication, as do dreams. Some readings were direct and precise, while others rambled from clause to clause, trapping the meaning in a net of words.

His readings varied in detail. Some told the general state of a patient's circulation, while others specified blood count and blood pressure. Readings of a given day maintained about the same level of detail, much as dreams of a given night are general impressions, while those of another night are sharply etched.

His readings varied in level of discourse, as dreams vary

from earthy material and even puns to poetic and spirited imagery. While most of Cayce's readings exhibited a stilted style, including the editorial "we," impersonal nouns such as "the entity" or "the body," and passive verb constructions, some included bits of slang, or the jargon of a trade, or a homely expression of the person he was counseling. On the other hand, some readings were rhapsodic, and the hushed and cadenced phrases of others might be scanned as poetry. These levels of discourse, Cayce insisted, had a lawful base, as did the same levels in dreams.

The Cayce readings varied in the breadth of their focus—just as some dreams are capsules or cameos, while others sweep in widening circles of imagery and insight until the dreamer has a perspective of startling magnitude. Most of the readings simply addressed the person and matter in hand, but there were days when the readings would swing easily into extra spontaneous materials. Such comments might be brief, perhaps telling the individual that his widowed mother would soon marry someone she did not as yet know. The comments might be lengthy, explaining a Biblical parallel to the problem confronting the person before him. Or the spontaneous comments might be made as though from another perspective, warning all who heard that God would not forever endure "a wicked and adulterous generation."

There were still other variations in the readings which could be paralleled in dreams. There were variations in how swiftly Cayce addressed the subject matter at hand, sometimes without waiting for the usual instructions—as a dreamer may fall asleep and suddenly be dreaming so deeply that when awakened he is disoriented. There were variations in Cayce's interruptions of what was read to him, as a voice interrupts a dream with a comment, or a dream scene yields to another. There were variations evident when Cayce gave a rare reading not yet requested, but needed by someone just then writing or telephoning him—much as dreams meet a need of others of which the dreamer is not yet consciously aware.

In all these variations, there were lawful modifiers at work, Cayce explained. For example, a whole series of modifiers within himself tended to affect his readings, just as the subjective state of the dreamer affects the form of his dream.

Cayce's health affected his readings. When he was ill he could not give them. When he was tired, they were less clear, detailed, or expansive. Similar factors, he said, affect dreams. Indeed, the effect of body processes on all types of dreaming is so real that one person's dreams over a period could be shown to vary according to whether he was on a vegetarian or a meat diet! Rest and physical fitness also constantly affect the recall, scope, depth, and clarity of dreams.

Cayce's state of mind affected his readings. When he was distraught and defensive with those about him, he experienced some of the few clear errors in a lifetime of giving readings: once in giving readings on oil wells, and once in giving readings on patients in his hospital. Neither time was a complete miss, but the distortions, as later readings pointed out, were dangerous; they contributed to his abandoning both the oil wells and the hospital.

His best readings came when he was buoyant, relaxed, humorous, secure. However, he also gave exceptional readings when in keen distress—as when he was twice jailed for giving readings, or when his university collapsed.

Dreams, too, he said, are conditioned subjectively. He urged his dreamers to get out and play, to take vacations, to balance up their wit and reason, to tease and to laugh and to enjoy children. But he also urged them to note the depth of dreams for the person confronted by death-loss, or by business failure, or by divorce, or by difficult vocational choices—all of which might call forth dreams of such depth and power as to make them "visions."

Cayce's readings were affected by what his own trance-products described as his relative "spirituality." When he was carried away by the ambitions of a treasure hunt, or temptations to seek notoriety with his gift and his considerable lecturing ability, he was reminded to notice how the quality of his readings suffered. On the other hand, when he was regular in his times of prayer and Bible study, as well as in his quiet fishing times, he was reminded to notice that his readings gained in quality, and that he even developed new types of gifts or capacities, both within his readings (for example, producing an entire series on a new subject), or awake (aiding the sick, through prayer).

Similar factors, his readings said, affect the quality of dreams. When his dreamers drove themselves for money or fame or power, they could see that their dreams brought up these very issues, and then began to deteriorate in clarity and helpfulness. When they were secure in their faith, their prayer times, and in their desire to serve others, they could find new vistas in their dreams—giving them glimpses into the world of the future or the past or the transcendent.

Besides the factors in Cayce's own personal life, there were more objective factors which influenced the form of his readings. While many people—perhaps almost anyone—could "conduct" a reading, the best guidance came with someone "passive"—not pushing for private ends. His wife fitted this role. In lesser degree, his readings were affected by the good spirits and spirituality of those in the room with him. The parallel in dreaming, as Cayce pointed out, lay in the effect on dreamers of their most intimate personal relationships. When husband and wife were bound in genuine love, dreams were facilitated by this bond and polarity, which often appeared in the dreams. Relations of brother with brother, or child with parent, would affect the stability and balance of the dreamer, and therefore the form and quality of his dreams. Such ties were not, he explained, matters of nice behavior, nor of duty, but of the weightiest significance to the soul itself.

Frequently, the Cayce source noted that the attitudes of those who sought information and guidance from Cayce affected what they got. Those who sought novelty, exploitation of others, a godlike guarantor for their lives, justification for their past mistakes, or anything but genuine aid and growth, received curt responses, or vague ones, or unexpected lectures on their motives. Those who failed to act on the counsel given them might find future counsel brief or even withheld.

Gullibility was as readily rejected as cynicism; adulation of Cayce accomplished as little as belittling or envy of him. "The real miracle," one reading said, "occurs in the seeker."

Similar factors, he said, govern the extent to which dreamers produce dream information helpful to those about them. Often a dreamer secures facts unavailable to a loved one because of his greater detachment toward the need or problem. Often, too, unconscious telepathy from a brother or sister or child shows dreamers how to reach the other's bad temper, or alcoholic habit, or despairing heart, or overbearing pride.

Glimpses of Lawful Patterns in Dream Interpretation

Just as there were lawful processes to color every reading Cayce gave, and every dream of every dreamer, so there were lawful processes of interpreting dreams.

Almost every dream reading, of the seven hundred that Edgar Cayce gave, began with a brief review of the progress of the dreamer. It examined how well he was recalling his dreams, how his waking experience of guidance and quickening paralleled his dreams, how the dreamer felt about his own progress, how far he had access to his own best self, what new gifts appeared in his dreams, how he handled old weaknesses, where he needed study or application, and how well he was interpreting his dreams without Cayce's aid.

All of these aspects of the dreamer's development, according to Cayce, can be reviewed for him in his own dreams. Indeed, one of the most frequent longer dream-types is the review dream, where one or more aspects of the dreamer's psyche or life is brought under scrutiny. Such dreams often go back to childhood, as their locale shows. Usually they involve many people, since the dreamer's identity and habits are bound up with particular people important to him. Or a dreamer might have an entire cycle of dreams, one every few nights, on the same theme—perhaps sex, or faith, or courage in adversity, or what to make of his talents. In general, as Cayce interpreted such review dreams, the endings indicate how the person is doing. A gloomy outcome and low spirits at the end underscore a warning, while adventure or discovery or attractive locales at the end underscore a promise.

As Cayce took up each dream in a typical dream reading, he first distinguished which levels of the psyche had produced that particular dream. The dreamer can also be taught by his own dreams, he said, to recognize the various levels working within him to produce each dream.

When a voice speaks in a dream, an aura of feelings and thoughts will show whether the voice is his best self or just his imagination. When a scene from the day flashes across his mind in sleep, he will be shown by nuances whether the scene represents merely worries from the day, or a prologue to helpful comments from the subconscious. When strange and outrageous material appears, his own subconscious will teach him to distinguish which is merely a dream caricature of his outrageous behavior, and which is instead a radical challenge to his being.

Dreamers should often ask in a dream, or immediately after it, he said, to be shown what part of their mentality has been at work in the dream, and why. Some of Cayce's dreamers were amazed at the colloquy which they were able to follow within them. Others were delighted to be able, they felt, to distinguish their own inner voice from the contribution of discarnates in dreams.

It was characteristic of Cayce's dream interpretation to set a small dream plot within a larger frame of meaning, when he felt that the dream intended it. A man who dreamed of the death of his brother, and was heartbroken, was shown the religious notes in the dream that distinguished it from a precognitive warning. The dreamer was seeing from his own superconscious, Cayce said, the meaning of the death of Christ, whom Cayce called the "elder Brother," for His fellows. A dreamer who saw himself escorting a strange young lady home from a dance was told to consider how service to others marked the full life. A businessman dreaming of a train trip was told it referred both to stock activity and to the question of the journey of the soul which he was studying at that time. In Cayce's view, dreams carry significant meaning on several levels at once, and should be interpreted accordingly.

Part of the art of interpreting dreams, according to Cayce, lies in the ancient art of "Urim," or recognizing symbols with relatively universal meaning. He emphasized the purely personal meaning of much dream contents, from articles of clothing to scenes of war. But he also challenged dreamers to see, in certain poetic and evocative dreams, the presence of symbols which have wide currency in myth and art. Fire often means anger. Light often means insight and help from the divine, as does movement upward. A child often means helpful beginnings, needing further aid from the dreamer. A horse and rider often mean a message from higher realms of consciousness. Pointed objects inserted in openings may well be sex symbols—although a key in a lock is more typically unlocking something in the dreamer.

Cayce used this kind of interpretation in less than twenty percent of the dreams he interpreted for most of his dream subjects, although more often in interpreting the dreams of his wife and a few others. The appropriateness of interpretation by Urim, he said, lay in the type of dreaming native to that dreamer.

In assigning to the term "Urim" the meaning of guidance by interpreting universal symbols in dream and vision, Cayce was incidentally solving a problem unresolved by Biblical scholars for generations—who have never agreed what sort of Old Testament divining it was.

One aspect of Cayce's dream interpretation was harder for dreamers to duplicate: the times he predicted their dreams, even the night and time of night. In the strange, wandering world of dreams, this bit of his skill seemed incredible—even allowing for the power of his suggestion upon the dreamer's unconscious. But he said he could do it because he could see factors in the dreamer's psyche which made the dreams inevitable, much as one on a high building could predict the collision of careening cars on separate streets below him. He added that dreamers would also learn to recognize when given dreams were signals of a new theme or series, and to predict for themselves how more would follow—as his dreamers did in lesser degree.

It was part of Cayce's skill in dream interpretation to devise analogies and illustrations for the point he said a dream sought to make. A dream scene on the simultaneous action of levels of consciousness is like seeing, he said, a pianist attending to sheet music and to finger action at the same time. The individuality of the soul, within its larger destiny, is like the individuality of a tree, coming from a seed and leaving one after it—true to pattern, yet a unique tree in itself. Cells sick in a body are like people who draw associates around them and start a movement with a mind of its own.

But this skill with images, a delightful part of the Cayce dream interpretation, is equally native to the dreamer, he insisted. This skill led to Frances' dream of canceling a trip to be with her baby, when she sought to understand her mother's care from the next plane of existence. It led another dreamer to see 1925 religious thought as a great hulk of a ship, foundering on a beach—beautifully built, but going nowhere.

In Cayce's view, determining the purpose of a dream is a major step in interpreting it. He explained that the psyche or total being tries to supply whatever the dreamer needs most. If the dreamer needs insight and understanding, it gives him lessons and even discourses. If he needs shaking up, it gives him experiences—beautiful or horrendous. If he needs information, it retrieves the facts for him. Dreams are part of a self-regulating, self-enhancing, self-training program, over which the dreamer's own soul ever presides.

An important step in interpreting a dream, then, is specifying what it came to accomplish—which the dreamer, according to Cayce, can learn to recognize for himself. A stock discussed by an acquaintance in a dream was a nudge to note and study the stock. But a stock seen in action, in actual figures, or described with instructions by a special kind of voice in his dream, was a signal for the dreamer to act, no longer to study.

Part of Cayce's training led dreamers to wake up after a vivid dream, review it in their minds so as to recall it later, and then return to sleep with the intention of having the dream interpreted for them—as it not infrequently was, whether by more episodes, or by essay-like passages, or by the voice of an interpreter or "interviewer," as one dreamer called it.

It is not surprising that those who studied hundreds of dreams with Edgar Cayce underwent major stress in their lives, and even marital or vocational crises. He showed them breath-taking vistas in their dreams, capacities for creativity which must have staggered them, and shaken their ego strength. He showed them that they could do whatever he did.

After the first few, Cayce never again trained dreamers as such. Instead, he trained people in an explicitly spiritual pilgrimage—one which included dreams but placed still greater weight on meditation, prayer, and daily service to others. Further, he trained people only in groups, where they could daily help one another in study, in love, in mutual intercession, in ways that his major dream subjects rarely knew.

But he insisted, whenever dreams or dream interpretation came up as part of this larger training, that dreamers could duplicate in the night—and sometimes in waking experiences—whatever he did in readings.

The Riddle of Outreach in Dreams

Cayce himself, when awake, wondered about the outreach that occurred in his readings and in his dreams. Accordingly, he dreamed about his question.

This dream, like a number he had, occurred while he was in trance, talking and concentrating on someone's need. A part of his mind was still available for a dream, even during a reading.

Shortly after the loss of his hospital, when he was asking himself the use of his gift after all, he reported the following:

> *Saw myself fixing to give a reading, and the process through which a reading was gotten. Someone described it to me.*
>
> *There was a center or spot from which, on going into the trance state, I would radiate upward. It began as a spiral, except there were rings all around—commencing very small, and as they went on up they got bigger and bigger. The spaces in between the rings were the various places of development which individuals had attained, from which I would attempt to gain information. That was why a very low developed body* [person] *might be so low that no one even giving* [psychic] *information would be able to give anything that would be worthwhile.*
>
> *There were certain portions of the country that produced their own radiation. For instance, it would be very much easier to give a reading for an individual who was in the radiation that had to do with health, or*

healing—not necessarily a hospital, but in a healing radiation—than it would be for an individual who was in purely a commercial radiation. I might be able to give a much better reading (as the illustration was made) for a person in Rochester, New York, than one in Chicago, Illinois, because the vibrations of Rochester were very much higher than the vibrations in Chicago. The closer the individual was to one of the rings, the easier it would be to get the information. An individual would, from any point in between, by their own desire to go toward the ring. If just curious (in seeking a reading), they would naturally draw down towards the center away from the ring, or in the spaces between the rings.

Cayce submitted this material for a reading, where he was told that it was an authentic vision of how his counsel was secured.

The vision had been correct in starting with Cayce as "a tiny speck, as it were, a mere grain of sand," for "in the affairs of the world" that was all Cayce was. Yet when he gave readings he was raising himself, or being raised, in a kind of funnel which stretched outwards and upwards until in its vast size it became all inclusive. He was being moved "direct to that which is felt by the experience of man as into the heavens itself." As he made his bodily activities "null" in trance, he was using only "as it were, (as seen in the cone), the trumpet of the universe—reaching out for that being sought." The answer to his reaching then came from the appropriate entity, some dot he had seen in its respective sphere, which "sent forth its note as a lute sends forth tones," to respond to his quest for information.

The reading was metaphoric, but its sense reached Cayce. It continued by assuring him that he had correctly seen how each individual, each group, each class or mass or nation, was found at some point on the vast spiral where its efforts had placed it, on the networks set by "an All Wise Creative Energy." Each speck was connected with the others, the reading said, as nerves connected each portion of a living organism to its center. Each could be instantly known or heard at the center.

He had also been correctly shown that the impact of

readings varied as they were given to seekers from Rochester or Chicago. But the difference was not in healing counsel, for that could be given as freely to one place and station as to another. The difference lay in the resonating which occurred within the individual, in his locale, as he received information and aid from Cayce. Each heard and responded as his circumstance and development allowed him to hear and respond.

From this time on, especially in life readings, Cayce often murmured as he began a reading, "High on the spiral of vibrations," or "Low on the spiral of time," or "This city has the same point on the spiral as Allentown, Pennsylvania." Others about him were not able, in his lifetime, to see the structure which these comments implied, but the structure was real to the sleeping Edgar Cayce.

He took this reading as assurance that it was possible for a man with human limitations and weaknesses (which his readings let him know were many) to enter a state of consciousness where much more than himself came into play to meet someone's need.

His readings took the same tack in explaining outreach to a dreamer, one of Cayce's main dream subjects, who reported an unforgettable dream experience of a loved one who had died. Cayce assured him that the experience had been an actual meeting. Then he listened patiently while the dreamer explained a diagram which he had drawn for himself, to show how people from different planes meet, where the plane intersects. Although he was unconscious, Cayce followed the diagram as though he could see it, and then proceeded to modify it.

The man should draw a star, he said. The triangular points reaching out were like the total psyche of each individual. Out at the tip was consciousness, touching and resting upon the person's body—even partly emerging from the body's network of senses and drives. But as one moved away from the tip of the point, the psyche broadened. And as one approached the part of the circle where the triangular shafts touched their neighbors, one had a visualization of telepathy, or attunement to those near in thought or concern. And at the place where each pointed structure opened into the center body of the star, there was the soul of that person—uniquely oriented to its own point, yet also ever present with the center of the star. Then, said Cayce (and here his analogy was like that of the spiral), the dreamer should contemplate how each individual might move in consciousness away from his own unique point towards the main body of the star, and into its center. The closer he got to the very center, then, the more he could enter completely into the consciousness and soul of each other person, or whatever plane of consciousness, represented by the other points of the stars.

There was a center in the universe, Cayce said. Indeed, a Center. Each man, each being, each creature and creation, was known and helped constantly from this Center.

He who, in dream or trance, drew near the Center, drew near to any other who needed him, or to any who could supply aid.

This was the answer to the riddle of outreach in dreams, however intricate the laws and processes involved.

To Edgar Cayce it seemed clear, however dubious to other serious men of his times, that man was not alone in the universe. And it seemed clear to him that the central Fact, bright as the center of a star, could be experienced as reality in dreams.

CHAPTER VII. HOW TO RECALL DREAMS

Edgar Cayce's readings were tailored to the individual who sought each reading—especially his dream readings, where he took up each dream personage and activity in terms of their meaning to the dreamer.

One person's dream of his brother might represent his own undeveloped side, corresponding to something he did not like in his brother. However, when the same brother dreamed of *him,* he might see a literal warning of his brother's health problem, not a representation symbol at all.

When a woman dreamed of a doctor, it might signal that her body was ready for conception. When her husband dreamed of the same doctor, it might be a subconscious evaluation of the singlemindedness of a dedicated doctor.

If Cayce saw dreams as so personal, did he also point to processes that might be learned by dreamers today?

How far to generalize on the counsel Cayce gave to dreamers in a question for research. Only when the processes he described for particular dreamers are understood, and can be repeated and varied, will we know how far his dreamers, and his counsel to them, were like other dreamers and the counsel they need today.

Such research has hardly begun. Only in the middle 60's have Cayce's readings been indexed and duplicated so that all those referring to dreams could be isolated and studied, together with relevant correspondence and case records. However, the outlines of his dream theories and procedures were evident to his close associates as early as the late 1920's, and they have continued to record and study their dreams, as well as encourage others to do so, along lines representative of Cayce's thought about dreams.

In particular, Cayce's son, Hugh Lynn Cayce, has fostered the development of scores of study groups which often use dreams, in the national membership society called the Association for Research and Enlightenment, formed before his father's death to explore phenomena and processes such as were discussed in his father's readings. Hugh Lynn Cayce and others whom he has trained (including Elsie Sechrist, author of *Dreams, Your Magic Mirror*), have taught for over thirty years hundreds of ordinary people to work with their dreams. These lay-explorers of the inner continent of the unconscious have not conducted laboratory research, but they have been naturalists of the country of dreams. Among their discoveries has been evidence on a number of Cayce's claims about dreams: that they contain ESP of many types, that they present material suggestive of reincarnation, that they are affected by prayer patterns, that they may contain a high order of mystical experiences of the divine, that the style of each one's dreaming is unique, that dreams may be made the basis for self-analysis by laymen.

Systematic research on the Cayce dream materials is also under way. At least one psychotherapist has reviewed scores of client dreams to see how they embody processes which Cayce described. And students in an advanced psychology course in dreams have begun comparing his dream interpretations with those of Jung and Freud. Experiments have been held by Hugh Lynn Cayce to test the effect on dreams of stimuli which the readings described: drugs, fasting, meditation, certain colored lights, telepathic sending of targets, and systematic self-analysis.

All of the preliminary work suggests that modern dreamers may indeed find guidance on the recall, interpretation, and application of dream material, along lines Cayce suggested in his readings.

Question: How Can One Learn To Recall Dreams?

Many have not recalled a dream for years, and some can never remember dreaming. Does this mean that they do not dream, or are not recalling dreams?

Cayce was careful to distinguish the dreams of normal, healthy and growing individuals from those with damage to the brain or other parts of the nervous endocrine systems. For the normal ones, as he saw it, there was no question that they were dreaming regularly, whether or not they recalled their dreams.

Long before modern sleep laboratories, where supposed non-dreamers are awakened when their eye muscles twitch, and helped to recall dreams at once, Cayce recalled for sleepers—on request—not only individual dreams but whole nights of dreams, and did so with such detail and force as to quicken the dreamer's own memory. After such experiences, the individual knew he was dreaming, and dreaming a great deal (as modern dream research shows about normal people).

Those whom Cayce coached had no great difficulty learning to recall dreams, once they set their minds to it. They had to be certain they were ready to confront whatever came forth in dreams, and to do something with it. Then they had to get across to their subconscious, one way or another, that they wanted dreams to be vivid enough to waken them, or to stay in consciousness in the morning. Some did it by telling themselves, just before dropping off to sleep, that they would dream and recall it—much as one tells himself to waken at five to go on a trip. Others did it by praying for guidance through their dreams. Others acquired the necessary first stimulus to recall dreams by reading and talking about them.

Cayce indicated, in one reading he gave on his own dreaming, that the body has a role in the recall of dreams. One can recover dreams better if he sets about remembering and recording them before he stirs his body, in the morning or when awakened at night. Evidently sufficient rest is also important, as Cayce repeatedly enjoined rest on those in dream-training with him—not only enough hours of rest, but the rest which comes easily with relaxation, exercise, fun, a change of pace, and committing one's life into God's hands.

He was firm with several dreamers that to recall their dreams they should record them—and go back over the records often. When he himself failed to record his dreams, Cayce was rebuked by readings for not using his mind on his dreams. (Part of the suggestion given him to secure dream interpretation included the "inquiring mind" of the dreamer; in one reading Cayce was himself told at the start that he was not "inquiring enough" about his dreams.) By the end of his life Cayce had made it a practice to discuss his more vivid dreams with his family, even if he did not write them out.

Cayce encouraged dreamers to start with whatever they could recall, even fragments. If they reported a hazy version, he corrected it. Yet he did less correcting for his systematic dreamers than a beginner might expect, for the dreamers soon learned that when doubtful, their own inclinations in recall were usually correct.

Starting with the moods on awakening could be useful, he reported. In his view, the individual's actions of the previous day, and of the current period of his life, are compared for him each night in sleep with his own deepest ideals. Accordingly, one who awakens grumpy and unrested ought to look into his life, as well as his dreams. And one who awakens in a clear and peaceful frame of mind may be sure that when he recalls his dreams they will not show him in serious inner conflict.

In Cayce's dream view, the processes of dreaming are not categorically different from those in waking life. While a dream may employ ESP to disclose the future or the distant or the unknown, so may a waking hunch or impression or inward voice. While a dream can unfold a dreamer's weaknesses of character, so can deep introspection. While a dream may offer an essay on the laws of consciousness so can a dreamer's hard study and incubation of them.

A dream may use a telltale image from the dreamer's past to convey a message, but so do waking memory-images and associations, as well as habitual word choices and slips of the tongue. So Cayce urged his dreamers to submit to him not only their dreams but also those happenings of daily life where the subconscious seemed to have the upper hand. And helping them with these, he also urged them to help themselves, by studying such waking products together with their dreams.

Finally, he saw it as important to the process of recalling dreams that dreamers act upon the dreams they recall. The very act of adding consciousness to the subconscious activity which produces the dream will set currents in motion within the total economy of the dreamer's mind—helpful currents to facilitate the recall of the next dreams, and eventually to aid in the interpretation of all dreams.

The simplest action is to record or tell a dream. This action is enhanced when the dreamer rehearses salient portions of the dream in his mind a number of times, whether he can interpret them or not. For if the dream reaches consciousness at all, it very likely has business with consciousness, and will profit from conscious attention. If the dream is a warning, going over it will strengthen the effect of the warning, however subtly. If an alerting, the effect of awaking and sensitizing the dreamer will be reinforced. If a lesson, rehearsing a dream will serve him as a drill.

Further, the remembered dream needs to be used, if possible. Not compulsively used, to be sure. But the subconscious is like a woodland spring to be dipped out and kept flowing, if it is best used. The dreamer may focus on some portion of the dream that strongly appeals to him, provided it is in keeping with his inmost ideal. For dreams, said Cayce, "are visions that can be crystallized." In dreams the real hopes and desires of the person, not idle wishes alone, are given body and force in the individual.

Trying to interpret the dream is better yet, for nothing

facilitates recall like a direct conscious hit or connection with an important dream content.

Interpretation, Cayce explained, is a matter of "weighing" the dream content with more familiar aspects of the dreamer's life and thought. Understanding always proceeds by comparison. The two major steps of interpreting the contents of dreams are grasping what the dream *refers* to and sensing the *trend* of the dream—what it seeks to change or to invest with new meaning. To interpret a dream, one compares the dream with his outward affairs, as well as his inward thoughts and feelings and intents. Sometimes the same dream plot refers to both. Growth in dream interpretation is growth in ability to associate comparisons to dreams, readily and aptly, getting the sense of the reference, and of the trend of the message or stimulus; a great deal of the Cayce training was his coaching in just this process.

Beyond interpreting a dream, one can improve recall by giving the subconscious action of the dream an even greater boost from consciousness. Study is one way—study of laws and processes that seem to be at work in the dream or in a series of dreams, and at work in the dreamer and his affairs. Like using two stars of the Big Dipper to sight the North Star, one can line up two or more similar dreams, and perhaps some waking reflections and happenings, to sight clear through to important knowledge about living: how the levels of the mind interact, how love draws love, how fear and doubt cripple, how concentration quickens ESP, how tasks of demanding service draw the aid of both the living and the dead, how prayer brings consciousness to a Center not its own. Books may help, and Cayce both suggested books to his dreamers, although few of them, and added explanations of the difficult passages they were studying in such works as Ouspensky's *Tertium Organum* or James' *Varieties of Religious Experience*. Yet the essential study is not books but experience, and above all the steady, slow unfoldment of the dreamer's psyche—where one can see by careful comparisons (not morbid introspection) all of the creative patterns at work that also govern nature and the realms of the spirit around them. It can even be said, Cayce affirmed, that all an individual can understand of the workings of God is what he can find at work within himself, as he responds to the rest of creation.

While study is a major step in adding consciousness to dreams, and therefore important for stimulating clearer dreaming and clearer recall, study alone is not enough. A more active response to the dream, or to a series of dreams, is equally critical in improving dream recall. Cayce called such action "application," and he included a section on application in every dream reading. Study is a form of application, to be sure, but he often had something more definite in mind. The dreamer must put his dream insights, tips, and quickenings into motion with muscle and nerve, trying out truths by experiment, in order to gain the full understanding and guidance that dreams offer. Over and over Cayce pounded this into his dreamers: "Do, do, do," he said to a man bemused with dreams.

Two kinds of action on dreams comprise the Cayce repertoire of critical applications: attunement and service. One can use dream states and experiences as guides to attunement with his highest self, touched in dreams, and to attunement with God as found in dreams. Or one can work from dream impressions toward attunement with his fellows, and even with the spirit of stocks and markets. This form of application should be practiced daily with dream material one has interpreted.

The second major mode of application is giving, serving. Providing for oneself and one's family is important, whether one is a sailor or a philosopher. But even more important, once the basic needs are met, is giving a hand to others less fortunate. In Cayce's view, service is not a nicety in life, and not an onerous duty. It is the hallmark of reality, the way of the soul which seeks to live in its birthright, not merely to drag through its days. The universe is so constructed that service is the chief end of man while on earth—bringing out in others, however one can, something of their best potential to glorify God. If this is done properly, under the guidance of constant attunement before each new step (and Cayce insisted on this), one does not have to manufacture himself in ever-improved models. His next becomings will arrive right on schedule, whether these include the handling of wealth or of medicine, or ideas or of inventions, of family or of enemies, of beauty or of justice.

Finally, Cayce believed one can facilitate dream recall, even beyond study and planned programs of action, by deliberately repeating the type of response a dream initiates. A prayerful dream state can be carried forward by systematic prayers—and the readings sometimes dictated to his dreamers (including Cayce himself) little prayers or affirmations which could be reworded and often used in the day. If a dream initiates a more loving attitude towards one's wife, one can not only understand the need for such love and make some decisions about it, but one can carry forth the action by daily walks with his wife. Not just being busy, but a celebrating, stretching, growing into the full force of the dream, are further steps in adding consciousness to dreams.

Each of these steps builds recall of dreams. They also build the depth and clarity of the dreams, for they serve to build the dreamer himself.

The alternative to recalling and interpreting dreams, said Cayce, is not always pleasant. Individuals cannot expect to drift forever. If they do not puzzle out their identity, and the direction of their lives by the aid of their dreams (which he said every normal person should try to do), then they may be brought, by the relentless action of their own pent-up souls, into some crisis which requires that they come to terms with themselves. It may be a medical crisis. It may be the end of a marriage or of a job. It may be depression or withdrawal. There are laws of this firm-handed disciplining, which he called part of "karma," or the process of sowing and reaping the harvest of one's deeds and thoughts, whether in one life or many.

Question: What Happens To Dreams Not Recalled?

Cayce made it clear, however, that even his most determined dream students were not recalling all of their dreams, and should not expect to do so. Many dreams are only meant to advance the dreamer's total growth, without reaching consciousness—nocturnal workouts which the psyche gives itself from the larger perspective of the subconscious, or from the yet larger perspective of the soul and of the Universal Forces. Such dreams do their work and go on.

Other dreams make a partial impression on consciousness, and are only partly recalled. If the dreamer is working at remembering and using his dreams, he need not be concerned about these fragments, for some are mere worry dreams, limited to consciousness and the levels of the mind closest to it, without helpful answers generated from the subconscious. Still other fragments, relatively few, serve to mask noise or body rhythms, and allowed the dreamer to keep on sleeping, as other such fragments do the opposite—wake him up when he should get up, without mysterious content. Further, there are food dreams not easy to recall, because while sometimes vivid, they have no "heads, tails, or points"—meandering nightmares, unlike those stark nightmares that certainly make their point and awaken the dreamer with it. In general, Cayce told his dreamers, a dream not fully recalled will repeat, with variations which do not change the reference or intent.

Cayce did not stress the "censor" effect in dreams, so much emphasized by Freud. It was obviously in operation in not a few of the dreams he interpreted, especially in dreams early in the study of a dreamer, before the dreamer had accepted the unpleasant or socially unacceptable sides of himself. Cayce preferred to point out that the petulance or lust or high-handedness often ascribed to another in the dream was really within the dreamer and projected onto others. But he did note a form of censoring that often occurred: his dreamers tended to forget or omit unpleasant or revealing parts of dreams more often than other parts; they also tended to forget happy endings, when the effect of such endings was to add to their sense of responsibility.

In addition to the question of dreams not recalled, Cayce addressed himself to the question of dreams known to the dreamer more by their actions on his body and emotions than on his mind. When the dreamer cries or screams or shouts in sleep, or walks or flails, he should be concerned for his general health, as he should when dreams are constantly and wildly unreal and unpleasant. In such cases, Cayce pointed out, the other imaginative processes of the dreamer are also likely to be affected: fantasy, daydreaming, and even the normal imaging of food or drink or companionship. Such distortion results from a physiological disability of the nervous system's sensory network, or of the autonomic nervous system that controls bodily emotions, or of both. Also, he commented in a score of readings on such dreams, the endocrine gland function of the dreamer is almost always involved and needs attention through action on poisons in the body, on failures in circulation, and on osteopathic lesions.

Dreams of the sick or fevered or damaged body, Cayce said, are not worth trying to recall and interpret. But most others which make their way to consciousness, leaving a clear plot and cast and mood, are worth the time to interpret. In 1924, when dream interpretation was used only by physicians for psychiatric purposes or by occultists for divination, Cayce was insisting that dreams are a normal aid by which the personality and body regulate themselves and advance the dreamer's affairs. They should be given, he emphasized, a larger place in the activities of "the human family."

Question: Are There Dangers In Recalling And Using Dreams?

Edgar Cayce saw dangers in *not* recalling and using dreams. Failure to do so might force the psyche to get in touch with itself by crisis or illness.

But he also saw dangers in recalling and using dreams.

The basic danger lies in the mind's powerful energies. These forces are not likely to be unleashed in the novice dreamer, nor in the person who keeps the levels within himself interacting by such non-dream processes as healthy prayer, artistic creation, honest loving, and hard work and play.

But one who seeks through dreams to arouse and tame the vigorous energies of the subconscious, without at the same time leading a sane and balanced, well-rounded life, puts himself in jeopardy.

Over and over Cayce warned his dreamers to keep their reason strong as they explored the land of dreams. They must continue responsible daily decisions, not relying on him or on dreams overmuch; on this he was adamant. They must continue to acquire skills and knowledge, the business of consciousness, as fast as they opened up the subconscious. A man must apply himself continuously to his work and thought, and a woman to her loving and relationships, however they were invited by dreams to new unfoldings.

As the farther reaches of dream experience opened up for his dreamers with experiences of ESP and of beauty and holiness, he told them even greater "equilibrium" was required of them, an "even keel," avoiding extremes of all sorts—whether of diet or thought or even of dream study. Otherwise, the same forces which operated so helpfully at one time would become destructive to the dreamer at another.

Dreamers might not only lose their capacity for guidance and growth by dreams—always a real possibility through narcissism, escapism, fanaticism, hypochondria, or messianism—but quicken dynamic energies within themselves which would not easily go away, seriously distorting and disturbing them if ignored or improperly used. In a revealing phrase, Cayce warned one dreamer that his selfish misuse of dream experiences, once they had begun to develop some stature and momentum in his psyche, would let loose "those disinterested forces" that could be harmful to the dreamer. The reference was not to discarnate entities, but to forces natural to the dreamer's psyche—as powerful as they were natural.

Yet dreams in general tailor their content to what the dreamer can effectively handle. They are self-regulatory and self-correcting. If the dreamer pays too much attention to dreaming, the dreams themselves draw his interest to daily affairs. If he lets himself become fascinated with one aspect of dreams, such as dream incursions into the land of death, he will find himself made foolish in just such dream settings until the point becomes obvious to him. But there is also a limit to the self-regulating in dreams. If the dreamer upsets his body or the balance of his whole psyche, he upsets the regulator function of dreams, and they run incoherently. Or he may impair this regulator function by strenuous suggestion to himself, before sleep and during semi-waking intervals in sleep.

Cayce was firm in warning against "forcing" dream experiences of any particular type. One should not run before walking, he told an enthusiast. One should trust his soul and his Maker to supply what he needed in the night, he told others. Working responsibly with dreams is not the same as forcing them to substitute for living.

In spite of the warnings which ran like bright threads through his dream counsel, one of Cayce's major dream subjects lost his balance in a period of mental illness which also contributed to the loss of his employment and his marriage. Another also lost his vocation and his family. Both lost their gifts and gave up using their dreams, which had made them millionaires and at times happy and productive people. Frances, too, had her troubles, as we have seen. But all were warned, as was the man who asked, "Will I be able to foretell my own death?", which he had seen enacted in a dream. The reading that day came in a tone of unusual elevation, which included promises of great service by the dreamer, if he were faithful, and warnings as well:

> *Then bind up thine feet, my son; keep thine ways aright, knowing there is the advocate with the Father . . . and when thou art called into account of those deeds done in the body, blessed will be found those that had come under the directing of thine endeavors! Keep—keep—the faith, the promise in thine self . . . keep in thee the guiding light to many a soul seeking the way.*

But then the reading added:

> *Be not overcome by much knowledge. Be not overdone nor undone by that as may be given [in dreams]. . . . Not of thine own power may these [prophesying] forces be done—for flesh and blood may manifest a spiritual truth, but may not order a spirit in any direction! Aid and succor may come through flesh and blood (in dreams or otherwise), even to those near the pit—yet there is fixed that impassable gulf. Rather he that makes his will one with the Father may be committed a special care through His direction. Keep that . . . and err not in well doing. Keep thine self close to Him . . . for the stumbling block always lies in self-aggrandizement of*

power and ability, stored up in one's own self, and in the misuse of self in relation one to another. Keep the faith, my son, keep the faith.

The counsel did not take effect. The dreamer, who had for nearly five years plumbed every potential of dreams and been told that his abilities could exceed those of Cayce, was soon alienated from his family and reduced to selling trinkets for a living.

Working with dreams, like all human activities which at times engage one's every level—like loving and fighting and holding power and rearing children and espousing truths and creating paintings—holds in it peril. The peril is there because the peril is in the human being. His unfathomed potential is always matched by the unfathomed freedom of his will. This is the Cayce picture of the danger in using dreams.

CHAPTER VIII. HOW TO START INTERPRETING DREAMS

As Edgar Cayce counseled more than sixty persons on their dreams, over a period of two decades, he uniformly encouraged them to interpret their own dreams.

However strange the dream materials, they were not, in his view, coming from an alien intelligence. Even when a dreamer's productions drew on greater wisdom than his own—on discarnates or on the Universal Forces—the dreamer was still viewing only what he could understand and was already beginning to live out. This meant there was always an inkling in the dreamer about each dream content, a little nudge of meaning that he could locate if he were patient.

But Cayce was less quick to encourage people to interpret dreams for others. To be sure, he told dreamers they could do whatever he did—and part of what he did was interpret dreams for others. But he treated this skill as unusual, and only encouraged one of his major dreamers in it—a man who dreamed of himself interpreting dreams for others! His interpretations, Cayce said, were in some cases quite sound, and could be even better, if he took the time to work on them.

Interpreting dreams, as Cayce described the process, is not looking up a symbol in a handy dream book and applying it to a dream. One interprets a *dreamer,* not a dream. That is why Cayce went to such trouble in every dream reading to specify which part of the dreamer's psyche was called into play by the dream, and what this part of the psyche sought to accomplish. If one grasps the dreamer in the dream, one can take the first important step in interpretation: determining which of the two major functions of dreams is to the fore in a particular dream—(a) problem-solving and adaptation to external affairs, or (b) awakening and alerting the dreamer to some new potential within him.

For most people, there is only one dreamer they grasp with the requisite depth: themselves. Accordingly, the proper study in dream interpretation is first of all oneself, at every level. Conscious plans, goals, interests, stances, decisions—all such elements need to be inventoried. The subconscious, too, should be studied, with its veiled habits, fears, longings, dependencies, defenses. Two more realms within call for study—the body, with its cycles, needs, habits, stresses, all of which might be mirrored in dreams; the soul, always present to the dreamer, and putting its imprint on him as his body does—but with its ideals, its searching questions, its burdensome memories hidden from direct view. Beyond the dreamer, yet resonating with him for his study and growth, is the realm of the Universal, with its energies and patterns reached by his superconscious.

"Study self, study self," was Cayce's first counsel on training to interpret dreams. He told people to search out memories, to list their working ideals in columns (physical, mental, spiritual), to decide what they honored in others and to compare this with themselves, to check their self-perception against what others perceived in them. He sent dreamers looking for laws, for the way X would appear whenever Y was present under Z conditions.

He was not fostering narcissism as he encouraged dream interpretation, for in later years when he trained people in groups, he specifically set them the task of talking over each other's dreams and visions—and then writing up the group's sense of what they had discovered. Working with others also working on dreams stimulated the psyche towards both helpful dreaming and helpful interpretation.

In these same groups he developed further the emphasis he had given to daily meditation on an affirmation, and deep silence. There is, he said, a frame of mind in which dream interpretation comes quickly and rings true. Often one can reach it by puzzling out a dream as far as consciousness would go— then praying about it and putting it down; when one picks up the dream again, in a quiet frame of mind, surprising clarity may emerge.

Bible study also stills the mind to a "oneness" with itself where dream meanings are transparent. Further, comparing dream incidents with specific Bible passages can awaken in a dreamer a sense of the big symbols, the "Urim" of the human family which repeats in dreams and myth, art and legend, of all ages. One of Cayce's most common coaching devices was to assign a dreamer a particular Bible passage to study with his dream. But he was also free, though he did it less commonly, to compare dreams with the experiences of Confucius, Moses, the Buddha, and Socrates, whom he treated with evident respect.

Whether a dreamer should also study books of dream theory seemed to Cayce to depend on the dreamer. He never discouraged it, and sometimes strongly enjoined it—especially on one dreamer with a sharp, curious mind. One of the strangest events in the entire body of Cayce readings occurred when this dreamer sought counsel on specific passages which he was reading—and got the comments immediately, although Cayce awake had never read the books. The experience may have somehow conveyed the thought of the books to the sleeping Cayce, for afterwards he occasionally illustrated points to other dreamers by referring to ideas from the same books —which he still had not read.

As when Cayce pulled from nowhere the names of medical specialists for physical readings, he also tapped, though less frequently—fields of scholarship. Explaining heredity and environment to one dreamer, he cited a study of scores of cases compared in hereditary chains, and encouraged the dreamer to read the book.

In all these ways, one can begin to train himself for the task of interpreting his own dreams.

But there was, of course, the question of interpreting dreams of a sick mind—which in Cayce's view always operated in a sick body. For these dreamers Cayce did not hesitate to recommend professional aid. He made it clear that professional aid had its limits, as when he told one dreamer that he was fixated on the idea of his own Oedipus complex, under the suggestion of his doctor. But he called for professional assistance to other dreamers promptly, in more than a dozen readings.

Question: Why Are Dreams So Confusing?

Edgar Cayce once dreamed that a watermelon was eating a pig. When he secured a reading on the dream, he was told that the ridiculous sight, just backwards from real life, was reflected the ridiculous way he was currently behaving. A plot that seemed meaningless made excellent satirical sense, once its purpose was established. In general, this is to be expected of dream material. All speech and thought, as Cayce described it, carries subtle nuances of association. A stranger will faintly resemble someone else. A predicament will be like one remembered, or one feared. A flag will carry a whole chain of half-recognized thoughts about one's country. In waking life these little associations are kept to the rear, so that communication occurs without distraction. In dreams, the associations come to the center of the stage.

Cayce told a broker that he dreamed of an old college friend because the friend was "bright" and studious—exactly the qualities the dreamer now had and needed in his work, studying a new phase of the market. He told a pregnant woman that she dreamed of a college girlfriend because of the girl's snobbish pride, representing her own airs about her forthcoming baby.

In waking life facts have association. In dreams, associations dictate the facts. Given this way of functioning, dreams are not so confusing after all.

Dreams originating with the subconscious, as it responds to the daily concerns of the dreamer, work up their plots and characters to present two things at the same time. They restate for the dreamer some conscious concern or interest of his, some decision or plan he is trying to make "deductively," based on all that he knows. At the same time they show him how that situation looks "inductively" when examined for the facts by the ESP of the subconscious. Given this complicated double task, it is surprising that dreams are not more confusing than they are. But sometimes even Cayce said of a dream episode, "Better let it go; it will come again" in a more intelligible version.

A dream of a talking spider taking over a man's house would seem absurd. Absurd, that is, unless one knew what Cayce saw instantly and the man's wife did not know, nor had the dreamer admitted to himself, that an extramarital relationship which had started on a small scale was moving to break up his home. Like a spider, it was spinning webs which were growing stronger and stronger. And the undermining comments of the paramour were doing deadly work, like the spider that talked. The only solution, Cayce told the dreamer, was the one in the dream: to cut the whole business out of his life, surgically and quickly. The dream went as follows:

I was standing in the back yard of my home—had my coat on. I felt something inside the cloth on the cuff of my left hand coat sleeve. I worked it out, but it was fastened in the cloth and broke off as it came out, leaving part in. It proved to be a cocoon and where it broke a small black spider came out. The cocoon was black and left a great number of eggs—small ones—on my coat sleeve, which I began to break and pull off. The spider grew fast and ran away, speaking plain English as it ran, but that I do not remember, except that it was saying something about its mother.

The next time I saw it, it was large black spider which I seemed to know was the same one grown up, almost as large as my fist—had a red spot on it, otherwise was a deep black. At this time it had gotten into my house and built a web all the way across the back, inside the house, and was comfortably watching me. I took a broom, knocked it down and out of the house, thinking I'd killed it, but it did more talking at that time. I remember putting my foot on it, and thought it was dead.

The next time I saw it, it had built a long web from the ground on the outside of the house in the back yard, near where I first got it out of my sleeve—and it was running up toward the eave fast when it saw me. I couldn't reach it but threw my straw hat in front of it and cut the web, and the spider fell to the ground, talking again, and that time I hacked it to pieces with my knife.

Cayce ended his reading on this dream by warning that aspects of the relationship "have grown to such extent as may present a menace to the very heart and soul . . . Beware! Beware!" His counsel was ineffective. The dreamer got the reading and left home, never to return.

Such a dream is confusing if one tries to interpret the dream alone. It is not confusing if one knows and interprets the dreamer, whose situation must be symbolized by something insidious, complacent, talkative, and repugnant.

A very different situation called forth another spider dream, this time from Cayce himself. He saw a drunk kicked into oblivion, who turned into a menacing spider. When he sought a reading on the dream, he was told it was one of a series on how to handle the criticism he was experiencing from people who considered his readings the work of the devil. Cayce's impulse was to strike back just as heartily as the dream depicted. But the consequence of retaliation is always to increase opposition, making it more deadly, as the dream depicted with the irresponsible drunk turning into a bearer of venom.

Yet Cayce recognized that the interpretation of dreams is no simple matter, precisely because people are not simple. As he talked about dreams in hundreds of readings, he pointed to four kinds of dream imagery: nonsense, literal, symbolic and visionary.

Question: How Do Dream Images Differ?

Nonsensical or meaningless imagery—like that which accompanies a fever—occurs when the body is reacting to its own stresses, rather than using images for self-regulation and self-enhancement. Cayce saw such material as produced chemically, from the blood stream, whether from alcohol produced by too many sweets, or the endocrine secretions that might produce a sex dream to accompany an ejaculation in the night. Such imagery was rarely interspersed with meaningful imagery in the same dream, but appeared in dreams or fragments of its own. When an erotic dreamer reported a fragment where a girl's hair brushed pleasantly against his face, Cayce said it was "just physical" and needed neither interpretation nor anxiety from the dreamer. However, when the same dreamer reported a complete dream which included girls singing naughty songs in his ear, Cayce analyzed this segment as important—showing how little thoughts of erotic fantasy catch the ear of the subconscious and build tendencies difficult to control.

Second in Cayce's explanation of dream imagery is a category more common in dreams than the nonsense imagery: literal imagery. As Cayce saw the function of dreams in normal people not under great stress, much of their dreaming serves the same ends as their conscious thought: solving problems of outward circumstances. If the dreamer's business is tending machines, he will dream about handling those machines. If his job requires him to hire salesmen, he will dream about qualifications of salesmen. If a woman is concerned about her baby's walking, she will dream of how to get him to walk. If she feels overshadowed by her husband's airs of self-importance, she will dream about his airs. If she worries about helping him in his business, she may dream of offering a lovely dinner party for his associates, or about going on the board of his firm—whatever is appropriate for her.

Yet literal imagery rarely stands alone. Among Cayce's dreamers, an accurate picture of the death of a friend's mother was also accompanied by symbolic material, suggesting how to view death and how to be helpful to the friend when death came. A precise literal picture of tomorrow morning's quotations on a given stock was often accompanied with a scene such as a rising elevator, to suggest the coming climb but the danger of getting too far off the ground in that stock. The literal and the dramatic are woven together, as Cayce interpreted dreams.

How, then, may the literal be identified in the midst of fantasy elements? Again, by interpreting the dreamer, not the dream alone. One must know the dreamer's conscious thoughts and enterprises to pick out literal dream contents mirroring his conscious concerns. Someone worried about a sick relative ought to consider a dream of that sick relative for literal elements. But someone provided by a dream with an imaginary sick relative or with a relative's illness from an exotic ailment, has less cause to look for literal health guidance. A man investing in stocks may expect literal dream comments on stock movements, but one who makes his money trading horses should expect literal dream material on horses, not stocks.

Despite the surprisingly large place Cayce gave to literal pieces within dreams, a place far in excess of that assigned by any psychologist or analyst in the century which rediscovered dreams, he still saw *most* dream content as symbolic, or "emblematic." In this respect he came nearer to the experts of laboratory and couch.

As Cayce saw dreams, their chief imagery is like figures of speech, pictured and acted out. Feet and shoes often have to do with one's footing, or foundation, in what he is attempting. Dreams of mouth and teeth often have to do with that annoying function of the mouth—speech. A dream of a headless man was, in one case, a blunt warning from the dreamer's subconscious not to lose his head in worries at his job.

But dreams are made less of conventional figures of speech than of personal figures—in the way that a commonplace tune will be forgotten by one man but will for another quicken the pulse with memory of a loved one and "our song." Every dreamer, in Cayce's view, has his own repertoire of personal symbols or emblems, loaded with shades of meaning displayed in dreams. Men who are more than a little fascinated with women found their temptations and their talents dramatized as women. Dreamers delighted and mystified by radio, in its early days, found in broadcasting imagery for both their messianic tendencies and their attunement to the unseen divine. A man interested in Warner Brother's stock at the advent of sound movies found that dream imagery of "Vitaphone" represented not only the excellent prospects of the stock, but also his need to rely on his inner voice for stock guidance—his own "vital phone."

Why do dreams employ emblematic material, instead of providing explicit guidance to the dreamer? Cayce reported that dreams are charged with accomplishing more than providing information and guidance. Over and over he insisted that dreams come to provide an "experience" to the dreamer. They are meant to make his heart pound, his knees quake, his spirit sing. They are "happenings" for the dreamer, not simply picture language. Seeing a stubborn bull, as Cayce himself did in a dream, occurred not only to tell him that he was bull-headed, but to help him feel for himself all the blind energy which made him shrink in the dream. Dreams are intended to *change* the dreamer somehow, not only to inform him. To accomplish both informing and transforming, dreams had to use emblems—materials which both signified and sizzled.

A dream of Cayce's where he saw the floor of a house cave in, disclosing a cemetery below, was not alone a message that he was building a current effort on a poor foundation; he was meant to feel the foundation as repugnant as a cemetery, and as dead and useless to him. A husband older than his wife who saw her swim a difficult lake to bring a prize to the other shore was not merely told to respect her, but helped to feel like cheering her, for the progress towards maturity that she was making. A spot on the shirt of a man dishonest in business was not only in the dream to recall his soiled behavior, but to reawaken in him his tarnished self-respect.

The fourth type of dream material, which Cayce often called "vision" or "visionary," is as strongly devoted to changing the dreamer as literal imagery is to informing him. Like emblems, this material contains both sense and punch, but the punch is to the fore, and radical. Cayce saw ordinary people as capable of dreams of great poetic power, however rarely, provided they are truly seeking to grow. Among those busy scenes that crowd the night will come a dream, from time to time, that seems to step from the pages of mythology or of scripture.

Such a dream was one of his own. It came two years after the loss of his hospital and university, when he was still struggling to discover the meaning of his gift and how he would make his living. It was part of a series of dreams, stretching over several years, that led him to put his trust in his Maker, rather than in wealthy donors or in the splash created by his own clairvoyance. It also accurately represented his own inward sense of mission about his life, in the conflict of more than personal forces. Yet it drew him at the climax to an intensely personal affirmation which he could share with others in his work. Its richness of detail accurately expressed a psyche which had made him not only a competent photographer but a prize-winning artist in photography.

I was on my way to a camp; had a strap over my shoulder with a little case which reminded me of a case for spyglasses, but I knew I had a message in it that I was to carry to whoever was the commander of the army where I was going.

The little box with a message was a symbol repeated in his dreams, representing his sense that he had something important to convey to people in the strange and awkward labor of speaking in trance. His dream continued:

It was rough climbing over the mountain.

This symbol, too, often appeared, and his readings called it the sense of his life journey, climbing upwards to better attunement with his Master.

I came down to the camp very early in the morning; it was just getting light. As I came down into the little ravine, I knew there was a stream of water not wider than a person could step over.

The symbol of fresh water repeated itself in his dreams, and he came to see it readily as what his readings called it—"the living water" of spirituality that must be offered to people by helping them where they needed it, as best he could.

I saw a host of men dressed in white: white shoes, trousers, coat and helmet. They each had two straps over their shoulders, one a large canteen-looking container.

Beings clothed in white symbolized for Cayce, as for others, those who were pure in service of the divine. The image had even appeared to him in waking visions, several times in his life.

> *And they were in groups of four, where they had a fire with a little skillet of some kind over the fire. They made the fire from something they poured out of the canteen; it looked like sawdust, but it was red, green and brown, and might have been ground cork or sawdust. Out of the other can they poured something onto the pan, and when they stirred it together it looked like an omelette, or just something good to eat, but I didn't know what it was. I saw no arms, guns, swords, or anything of the kind, yet I knew it was an army.*

The image of a warrior for the Lord was also one so strong for Cayce that it appeared to him at least once in a waking vision.

> *I didn't know anyone, but all up and down the ravine I could see the people preparing their breakfast in groups of four. And I asked them where the man in charge was. His tent was farther up or down the ravine. I could see a great white tent in the distance.*

It was not the only time he dreamed of being led to the unseen person in charge.

> *One here and there joined in showing me the way to go. After a while I came to a place where, over to the right, there was another little ravine that turned off to the right. And as we got just opposite this (myself, and those that had come following me), we heard from out in the darkness someone walking on the sticks. We could hear the sticks break, and we stopped to listen.*

There appeared a host of people dressed in dark; not dark skin, but their clothing was dark, not black but dark gray, browns, and the like. All their wrappings were dark.

It was typical of Cayce that he saw "the legions of darkness" not as black, but only darkly clad. Awake or asleep, conscious or in trance, he struggled with people whom he felt were wrong or misguided, but they were not for him monsters—only in the dark. His was not a black and white, paranoid cosmos, however genuine its divisions.

Then an angel of light stood between us, so that we could not see the crowd or group of dark people.

The angel symbol was as familiar to Cayce as his well-read Bible. Yet there was nothing trite for him about the concept, both because of a few intense visions he had experienced in his lifetime, and because of the awe that touched even his readings those few times when the subject of angels came to the fore.

Then there appeared the angel of darkness. The angels' figures were very much larger than ours as men—taller, heavier: of course, their countenance was very much brighter. When the angel of darkness appeared, he was dark like the people he was leading, but very much larger. His wings were something like bat wings, yet I knew that they were neither feathers nor just flesh, but the means of going fast wherever desired.

The imagination of an artistic photographer was clearly engaged. Cayce was having an experience, not just contemplating an idea in his dream.

The wings appeared to be from the loins to the shoulders, rather than just something growing out of the body—both in the angel of darkness and the angel of light. The angel of light had wings something like doves' wings, but extending from the loins to the shoulders, leaving his arms and legs free.

Now the action began.

The angel of darkness insisted that he (the angel of light) should not stand in the way, but demanded that there be a fight between someone he would choose and one that the angel of darkness would choose. Then there was between the two hosts a place cleared away, something like an arena, and I was chosen as the one to fight with the hosts from darkness. And we were wrestling.

I felt that I hadn't delivered my message and I didn't know just what I would do about it—that I had waited so long and I hadn't told them what I had come for, and I wondered why they had chosen me.

Cayce's poignant anxieties about his life, his gift, his message, showed here. He could not guess that in less than two years he would be momentarily jailed in Detroit for practicing medicine without a license. At the moment his waking anxieties were more on money matters—even just getting enough for him and his family to eat, as some of his dreams had shown.

I could still feel the strap and little package. I only had the one package, and wondered why I hadn't been hungry, as the others seemed to have to eat, but I only had the message to carry.

Then I began to wonder if my strength was to fail me—if the imp or child of darkness was to put me down in the dirt. It would be an awful thing.

Part of Cayce's experience under stress, as his dreams clearly showed, was not only a tendency to depression, but a tendency to want to respond to the attractive women who often surrounded him. It was a tendency he fought with a lively sense of its reality and its potential danger, to both his family and his work or "message."

But I knew if I could remember one word to say that he couldn't; and I tried and tried to think and couldn't find it. I couldn't remember what had been written in the message that I was to take.

Finally, as if just from out of the center of me, there came the words which I spoke aloud: "And Lo, I am with you always, even unto the end of the world!" As I said that, everyone of the darkness fell back, and there was a great shout that went up and down the ravine from the people in white. And as they fell back, the leader or angel of darkness (as the one that I was wrestling with fell away) reached out his left hand and struck me on my left hip.

That woke me; and I had an awful pain in my hip.

The closing flourish of his dream bore unmistakable resemblance to the biblical dream of Jacob wrestling with the angel. It also disclosed Cayce as aware that he was not, nor would be, a man of perfect behavior and virtue, but one touched and pained by darkness just as others were—an accurate estimate in his other dreams.

But the heart of the vision was the Biblical quotation which came as from the center of his being, defining his work as more than a psychic novelty: a means of awakening people to the unfailing presence of God. Yet to say it, to "deliver his message," by his words and his life, Cayce had to be conscious of his central thought, right in the middle of his own distresses. If his message did not apply to him in his own uncertainty and financial straits, how was he to give it to others?

In this vision, the central thought had not been so different from that which had struck him while awake, when two years previously he had lost his hospital and felt like dying—as his readings told him. Then one day, he reported, "While in church, the words in the song book spoke to me and danced right before my eyes. The words 'My grace is sufficient for thee' seemed to be impressed upon me."

Few of Cayce's dreams and few dreams of those he counseled were as stark as his symbolic dream of the legions of light and darkness, with his own small but sturdy case carrying the right thought for him and for those few who followed him. Yet such dreams occurred, and Cayce gave them weight.

Were such dreams the expression of mental illness?

One had to interpret the dreamer, not just the dream. If Cayce's life were organized around religious motifs, and if he felt under keen distress in vocation, perhaps such symbols were fitting, and not sick. In his life at another time, when he was a successful oilman staying in the best hotels, these symbols might have had a different and more ominous quality. Then he might have heard from his readings the kind of rebuke that one of his dreamers heard, who reported a dream experience that went, "Buy or sell five hundred shares of General Motors. I am the Lord your God."

That the dreamer was not receiving divine guidance, said Cayce in his reading, was obvious from the fact that the instructions on whether to buy or sell were not clear. He warned the dreamer that such a dream pointed to lack of balance in both understanding and actions in the dreamer's life. The line between divine aid and mental illness might be a fine one, but it was there. It was in fact—in the words already quoted on a dreamer's ambition to impress others by predicting his own death—"an impassable gulf." Not every vast symbolic content was meant to hearten the dreamer; it could also appear as a stark caricature of the dreamer's own pretentiousness.

Given the uncertainty about interpretation of every kind of dream content, can one ever be sure of dream interpretation?

Question: Is It Possible To Be Sure of Dream Interpretation?

Cayce's first answer to this question was in keeping with his emphasis on the role of "experience" in dreams. If the function of many dreams is to move the dreamer forward in his total life and growth, then such movement is an important function of interpretation, as well. A poor interpretation which gets only part of the dream's sense, but sets the dreamer thinking about an important aspect of his life, is not such a poor interpretation after all. Cayce set more store on advancement than announcement.

But of course those who tried to interpret their dreams with help wanted reliable means for validating their interpretations. He offered three such means.

The first is comparison within one's dream records as such. More often than not, several dreams of a given night focus on the same question or problem or awakening. What is clear about one dream ought to shed helpful light on others of the same night. Certainly the successive episodes of the same dream, however illogically connected on the surface, ought to be examined for the same motifs, whether shown over and over again, or expanded upon in segments. And interpretations for one dream ought to be compared with past interpretations for similar dreams. Frequently Cayce used in his readings the phrase "as has been seen," to refer to previous dreams, and to invite the dreamer to interpret in the light of his whole body of recorded dreams, rather than shooting at one dream at a time.

Dream interpretations can and should be validated in part by comparison with earlier dream materials for changes. If a theme is often repeated, it is likely that the dreamer hasn't yet caught the point—or acted on it. But if a theme shows a progression in successive dreams—for example a tempering of sexual rapacity with respect for the lover—then the dreamer might conclude that he is both interpreting the dream material effectively and making progress on the forces within himself that produces the dreams.

Secondly, a dreamer may validate his interpretations by comparing them with his subjective impressions about the interpretations. A feeling of release from inner panic may signal a sound interpretation, however unpleasant the truth the dreamer must face. A sense of heightened alertness, being keyed up without undue fear, may indicate that one has correctly come upon a warning of something untoward in outward affairs, foreshadowed in the dream. Relative certitude of interpretation may follow upon seeing how a given theme repeats itself in a series of dreams—for psychological certitude comes of stable repetition, from sensing lawful processes, according to Cayce. And the forceful quickening of new resolution or feelings, new stances in life, may also signal that one has struck upon the essential message of a dream.

Cayce encouraged his dreamers to rely on "the still small voice within," once they had learned to distinguish this voice from the clamor of conscience or anxiety or rationalization. It was a voice they could use, whether for guidance in dream interpretation, or guidance in driving a car or a bargain or an argument.

Thirdly, Cayce offered his dreamers a more comprehensive test of the validity of their interpretations. He told them to look at the quality of their lives. If they were growing, if they were functioning effectively in their rounds of life, the chances were that they were understanding and working with, rather than against, the mainstream of dream contents.

The test of their lives might be as simple as how grumpy they were. But better then examining their own lives, to approve or disapprove themselves, was to examine the quality of their relationships. Cayce never wearied of stressing the absolute importance of "the fruits of the spirit" in determining the forward-moving quality of a life. Patience, kindness, helpfulness, forbearance—these are not marks of a weakly feminine character according to Cayce, but of one who has found himself and his Maker, and does not project his fears onto others. The dreamer whose close associates—his family and his relatives and his business associates—give him their approval day by day is a dreamer who has the best overall test, however general, of the validity of his work with his dreams. These are the people who populate most dreams, Cayce said, just because they are the ones to whom a dreamer's being and behavior are most clearly known.

Nor are practical daily life skills to be ignored, in this way of estimating the validity of dream interpretations. When working well with his dreams, a dreamer ought to play golf better, Cayce said about one dream. He ought to make better business decisions, ought to make better speeches, ought to make better money—all other circumstances being the same. A woman ought to find herself more alert to dangers and illnesses for those in her charge. She ought to dress with better taste, entertain better, reason better about politics or religions, shop better, and supervise employees better—all matters in which he showed dreamers they were helped by their dreams.

And finally, as part of his third type of validation by the thrust and quality of a dreamer's life, he told his dreamers they could rely on the evaluations made by those who covenanted with them in a spiritual-search group, such as Cayce encouraged for all dreamers in his post-hospital days. Those who met with a dreamer to talk honestly and deeply, week after week, about the real fabrics of their lives, would not be easily nor totally fooled about him, especially if they prayed for one another daily, as they should. Dream interpretations could be tried out on them, for group members could interpret his life, not just his dream.

Question: How Can The Usefulness Of Dreams Be Improved?

Few of Cayce's claims to the dreamers he coached were better verified than his claim that their dreams would change as they worked on them.

The dreams changed in length. First came snatches. Then for a while came long, rambling dreams, as though the dreamer were walking over the grounds of his inner estate. Then the dreams developed sharper definition. Partly this happened because the dreamers could sense the important dreams to recall and submit to Cayce. But partly their very psyches seemed to set forth the desired dream content and experience in sharper form, in terse comments, in scenes which carried with them interpretive thoughts.

The dreams also contained more religious experience, as they unfolded over a period of years. Part of this change may have reflected Cayce's own orientation. Part of it may have come from the stress under which a dreamer was placed by discovering that he could dream of stocks, or of meeting the dead, or of past lives, or of sickness and cures. To do this in American culture was strange, whatever it might reputedly be in Tibet, and raised questions of life's ultimates, for the dreamer. But part of the change may have come from the dreamer's own clarity of mind, and the ability of his soul or his superconscious to get through to him, after he had dealt with the pressures of more immediate subconscious material.

The dreams showed a tendency to go over familiar

themes at deeper and deeper levels. A man whose early sex dreams largely emphasized controls found the theme of sex recurring in a series of dreams many months later which emphasized compassion along with passion. Then, still later, there were dreams followed by one searching review of his entire sex life, where a voice explained at the end that the crowning of masculinity was the giving of seed to others, seed for their total growth; it was the Greek idea of the Logos Spermatikos developed in the dreams of a twentieth century businessman without a classical education (but one who had, said Cayce, been a Greek in a past life).

The dreams showed cycles which analysts have noted, by alternating periods of weeks or months where they built up the dreamer, with other periods during which they took him apart. It was as though the psyche systematically raised him to new plateaus of maturity, and then relentlessly ground on his impurities until time to move him again.

A striking feature of one man's dream record was the emergence of a voice which spoke to him in dreams, making the major point of a dream, commenting on dream scenes, or simply instructing the major point of a dream, commenting on dream scenes, or simply instructing or rebuking him. Others also had this phenomenon, but never as dramatically as he.

Cayce insisted that each person's way of dreaming is as individual as his fingerprint—or as the markings of the soul in its long journey through many lives.

Yet another form of change lay in the closeness of dreams to waking impressions. One who dreamed of talking with the dead on another plane began to sense their presence and thoughts at moments of quiet while awake. A man who dreamed of stock movements before they occurred also began to sense, in hectic trading on the floor of the exchange, what would happen next to particular stocks. A mother who dreamed of her baby's health needs began to know awake and with accuracy when he was ill and when just fitful. A young man who was shy and argumentative with strangers came not only to dream about how to relate to each one in turn, but to feel spontaneous promptings on how to approach people and to listen to them.

A noteworthy change in dreams that occurred over several years of study was the shift to concerns larger than the dreamer's own personal affairs. Political questions, religious trends, the needs of undeveloped nations, the conflict of modern values, the long journey of the soul, the control of disease epidemics—these matters began to come into dream focus. It was as though the dreamer were making his way through his own layers, down to the strata that he shared with others in his time. To be sure, Cayce said that the issues which emerged in this fashion were colored by the dreamer's interests developed in past lives. But he did not minimize the importance of transpersonal dreaming, once the dreamer had taken firm hold upon his own life. On the contrary, he gave such dreams vigorous attention, for they fitted into his own insistence that no life was fully lived which was not lived for others.

Finally, the dreams of those Cayce coached offered them new experiences over the years. Some of these experiences were radical. When one dreamer first met in dream a parent who had died, the dreamer was shaken for weeks. The effect was even greater when the dreamers had their rare but decisive experiences of meeting Christ in dreams. But even the experience of inspecting the exact thoughts and feelings of someone living left its mark upon them.

Other new experiences were less startling and more adventurous: glimpsing a scene from a past life; getting a drawing of an invention; surveying a dream seascape of radiant beauty; discovering that two had dreamed the same dream on the same night; dreaming the location and type of trunk in which treasure was buried; dreaming of a friend just before he arrived.

Typically the "new experience" dream signaled the addition of this type of dream to the permanent repertoire of the dreamer. From then on, he might dream in these terms at any time. In fact, he was likely to. For once the psyche has opened the door to a particular type of dreaming, it seems to program a series of such dreams, to train the dreamer in the new type of dreaming—provided that the dreamer wants to dream in this way. Choice seems to be at work in dream types. Cayce told a woman who screamed in fright when she saw her dead brother in a dream that she need not be afraid, such dreams would not recur if she did not want them—or secretly seek them for their novelty and thrill, in some corner of her mind.

If dreams change so markedly, over the periods of time in which they are studied and used, can they be deliberately cultivated?

Cayce's first answer to the question of cultivating clearer and more helpful dreams was always the same: use the dreams. One lover of photography who saw himself entering his darkroom and finding his safety light shattered on the floor was told flatly that his guiding inner light would go out if he did not use it more faithfully. Among Cayce's earnestly repeated warnings was, "To know and not to do is sin." A dreamer who saw ancient warriors girded for battle, but feasting indolently on fruit delicacies, was told that his own inaction on dream promptings was making him look just as ridiculous to his own higher self.

Yet neither blind activity nor compulsive dream study, Cayce said, will improve the quality of dreams. Every person who seeks to grow, whether in dreams or awake, must find and assess his own working ideals. Words are not enough. One can profess love of God but only mean to flatter Him, said Cayce in a reading where he challenged a dreamer to distinguish between the deep cry, "As the hart panteth after the water brooks, so panteth my soul after Thee, O God" from the prudent affirmation "I know that Thou art a righteous God, rewarding them that seek Thy face." All the difference between a great ideal and a shabby one can be found in those two Biblical quotations. The ideals that matter are located in the tough pinches of life—in power, in wealth, in fame, in death, in sex; what did the dreamer really think and do about these things, and why? Was his ideal really his own, born of reflection and decision and more reflection? Or was it merely convention?

Once one clarifies his own deepest ideal, however hard to word and to picture, he must begin lining up his psyche in harmony with it, or his dreams will show him in constant conflict with himself. Part of lining up the psyche with its ideal, and ultimately with its Maker, is laying aside fear born of past mistakes. There is indeed a healthy fear that a soul should have, said Cayce, if it turns its back repeatedly on the best it knows. But morbid dwelling on past mistakes and excesses has no place in a program of improving dreams. Cayce was firm about this, resisting self-condemnation whenever he saw it, and insisting that guilt be replaced with present action. In one of his more startling sayings, he told a dreamer with unpleasant memories of sexual indulgence at the expense of the women in his life that "no condition is ever lost." Whatever the failing, even the cruelty, if the dreamer puts his life squarely in the hands of the best he knows, he will find his bitter fruits being turned, over the years, to the wine of understanding for others. What has been one's "stumbling-block," he often said, can be made his very "stepping-stone" towards love and aid to others, because of deep sensitizing action—provided that the psyche is oriented to allow this transmutation to occur.

Cayce taught his dreamers other broad procedures. They were to work out their own philosophy of life, so that their whole minds might operate with conviction, right down through the subconscious to the soul. They were to carry forward the sense of dream symbols in the symbols they used in waking life—from the decor of an office to the symbolic "life seals" they might fashion for their walls as a kind of soul crest. They were to study new types of dreaming, soak in big symbols from ancient cultures, pray for guidance on particular dream contents, record their waking impressions on the same day they dreamed a certain theme. He also taught them knacks of interpretation by precept and by example. One should, as he did, seek first the overall thrust of a dream. Did it end happily or unpleasantly? What was the overall attitude or mood which it brought forth in the dreamer, and why might this be appropriate? A dreamer saw a Jewish friend forcing his wife to sing Christian hymns. Cayce told him that he should have little trouble seeing, in this dream, his own tendencies to force convictions on family members.

What choice did the dream present, if any? A man saw himself in a dream planning to shoot off fireworks to entertain the girls at the beach, but the fireworks were taken and set off by another, who won the applause of the onlookers, while the dreamer was disconsolate. Yet as the dreamer watched the fireworks, his attention was caught by the beauty of the sparks that lasted against the sky and were mirrored in the ancient ocean. The choice, Cayce said, was one which would occur often: to play for applause of his fellows, or to keep his eye on the sparks of the eternal which he could trace in his fellows and in all of creation. A husband found himself in a dream following an attractive girl as she swayed her hips in a suggestive walk down the street; yet he also noticed that when she called a cab, she knew exactly where she was going, and resisted advances made to her. Which way of relating to others was the dreamer going to follow, Cayce asked? A path of seduction, or a path of knowing his purposes so well that others were attracted rather than distracted?

Not all dream references need be complicated. Cayce himself dreamed of Solomon and was promptly told in a reading to seek Solomon's wisdom, but without his fondness for women. A woman who dreamed of herself on a ship in a fog was told that she was truly "all at sea" in her life. A businessman seeing two figures in a dream, one stout and one lean, was told he had dreamed a cartoon of two attitudes toward a situation in his work: fat optimism and lean pessimism.

But the note which recurred like a silver thread in Cayce's seven hundred dream readings, whenever he explained to others how to improve their dreaming and interpretation of dreams, was a familiar one in every type of Cayce reading—medical, life, business, topical. That note was service.

For some dreamers, service through dreaming meant literally dreaming for others and giving them aid and counsel. But such dreamers were few among those who consulted Cayce. Others were encouraged to draw or to write stories based on their dreams. Or to share stock tips secured from their dreams. Or to learn from their dreams the laws of human development, and teach these laws to classes of interested adults. Or to teach others to dream. Or to pray for those presented to them in their dreams. Each one's gifts were different.

Whatever the gift, Cayce said, there is a law about its development which applies alike to all gifts. Its first application must be to those closest to the dreamer. If one can't be loving to his wife, no dream can help him quicken love in others. If one cannot teach his children the fundamentals of living, there is no point in his preaching them further. If one cannot guide a partner in a business choice, through dreams, one cannot expect to guide the government. It is the way of growth. First the dreamer must change and grow. Then he must find a way to share his growth in unassuming service to those closest to him in everyday life. Only then may he find dreams that can occasionally help the leaders in his profession, or his social class, or his school of art, or his reform movement—by helping him to help them.

It is a law underscored by the failure of the early dreamers that Cayce trained to sustain the high potential which he saw for them, and which they realized at times in both their dreams and their lives. They fell away from one another in their families. This was a blow the straining psyche could not survive, said Cayce, while it was reaching for the heights of dreaming. With his next dreamers he put his first emphasis not on dreaming skill at all, but on loving and producing. There was loving and producing in the family, there was loving and producing in the daily work, there was loving and producing in the gathered fellowship of those who met to study and pray. Only this course—the course of giving, giving, giving—would keep the flow of dreams clean and ever stronger.

His judgment proved sound. Under this kind of coaching, housewives became authors—and stayed good wives. A sea captain became an administrator of a research society—and stayed a good sea captain. A scoutmaster became a trainer in group dynamics—and kept his humor. A schoolteacher became a prayer leader—and a better teacher. A stenographer became a curator of ESP records—and learned to manage other stenographers. A mother became a psychic—and stayed a good mother. Each of these people worked with their dreams, and worked hard on them, for years. None of them tore the fabric of their lives.

If Cayce's dreamers were to grow in dreaming, they had to grow together.

PART III. ESP IN DREAMS

CHAPTER IX. DREAMS OF THE FUTURE AND THE UNKNOWN PRESENT

The century of the rediscovery of dreams has also been the century of scientific investigation of psychic phenomena.

Two kinds of investigation have filled library shelves with books and journals on telepathy, clairvoyance, mediumship, psychokinesis, survival of death, dowsing, drug-induced visions, and animal homing. One type has been the collecting of spontaneous experiences—the work of naturalists of the mind. The other type has been the establishment of lawful variations in the phenomena—the work of laboratory researchers. Both types have produced staggering amounts of data.

Yet psychic experience cannot be called a fact of science. The first and most important reason is lack of an adequate theory. Until it can be shown exactly how psychic phenomena work, how they start and vary and stop, the findings remain suggestive data. Theory is also needed to tie psychic happenings with better-known phenomena of the mind—with memory, emotion, perception, and learning.

A second reason for the dubious modern status of psychic phenomena is that they are often associated with a philosophy of dualism—of two basic substances called "matter" and "mind"—which is a philosophy uncongenial with modern scientific thought.

A third reason for their dubious status is the fact that they have not yet been sufficiently tamed to put them to practical use. Science can handle strange processes, provided it can show results—as the history of psychoanalysis shows.

But the cool reception accorded to psychic phenomena

in modern times has not banished the report of them. Edgar Cayce was largely snubbed by scientists in his time, yet he went on giving his readings—whatever they were. And his readings kept insisting that psychic phenomena were lawful natural processes which could be studied, duplicated, and applied. Especially in dreams.

Dreaming of the Future

By the late 1920's, no dream of the future might have been more valued by an investor than advance aid on the great stock crash of October 1929, which initiated the Depression and wiped out fortunes. Since Cayce's major dreamers were at work during the years preceding this stock collapse, they had a firsthand opportunity to use dreams to protect themselves.

The first hint of the 1929 crash came in late 1927, when one of the dreamers reported to Cayce a type of dream that had now become familiar to him: a voice or "interviewer" from his own subconscious and superconscious talked with him.

> *An interview in which I was told that something was taking place or would take place in Steel, that would lead to a two-year bear or liquidating market, in which U.S. Steel would go up only 5 points at the end of or during the course of 2 years.*

While Cayce often called the counsel of the interviewer literal, he also reported that stock details could be symbolic—as in this dream. What the dreamer was seeing ahead for two years was his own chance to "liquidate" or make money on stock guidance from his "interviewer" or inner voice for that period. But with it went a warning, that if he did not use his ESP ability effectively for the coming two years, he would not have an opportunity to do so again until the "five-point" or "five-year" lapse had occurred. In other words, the dreamer had until 1929 to make extensive money on stocks through dreams, or he would find himself waiting until 1932 to again make significant gains.

A couple of weeks later, he dreamed further within this timetable of the future.

Interviewer: "The conditions will last for one year and a half." My reply: "I don't find the conditions." Interviewer: "No, you don't see them now, but you will find them."

Interpreting the dream, Cayce urged the dreamer to think back to how he had been worrying about securing funds to establish the Cayce Hospital. The dream had followed with an answer to this concern. The substance of the assurance, Cayce said, was that for eighteen months the dreamer would continue to be anxious about funds, and that at the end of that time (early in 1929), "great will be the inflow from many sources," for "in great numbers, great quantities, shall be the means to carry on." But Cayce was clear that the promise of much money did not extend beyond the period. As it turned out, the dreamer and Cayce were both correct. There were eighteen more months of hard work. Then, early in 1929, the money began to pour in. The dreamers were soon millionaires and Cayce had large stock accounts; the hospital was established that year and plans laid for the university. It was the time of greatest wealth in Cayce's career.

Then exactly a year before the crash, a dream about Montgomery Ward stock led the dreamer to ask about "the general slump" which he felt was coming. Cayce confirmed that there would be a "general break" which would begin in rails, but that if the dreamer and his associates would continue to stick to their inner guidance, they would by then have "power and affluence."

In January of 1929, a dream of stock guidance from his dead father led one dreamer to ask, "Does this mean that we should sell out everything? What would be a good time to do it?" Cayce assured him that his father had only shown him the start of the break to come later that year. In the same night came a warning to the dreamer about messages he was seeking through a medium. The source was contrasted with the dreamer's father, whose dream messages he had learned to trust.

I was sitting in school with my brother. The teacher was there. He asked us some questions. I answered a question and said, "I'm in partners with my brother on the Stock Exchange." My brother interrupted in irritable fashion, saying, "That's Pop." Then the teacher showed me a very ugly looking individual, rather ferocious-looking sort of person. All the others cleared away. The teacher gave me a glove turned inside out. Inside that glove was protection against the individual. We ran out into the hall trying to escape. It seemed to be a shrewed sort of individual—tried to misrepresent himself.

According to Cayce, the dreamer had correctly seen a lesson—as suggested by the school setting—that there were discarnates who would give questionable guidance through a medium, even though they might at times give factual guidance. He warned that the two brothers might be "led astray" by such "misrepresenting of the various phases of phenomena," and urged them seek protection or "covering" from "inside," represented by the glove—meaning inward attunement with the divine, not with discarnates alone.

It was mediumism which eventually led them into trouble in their stock activity, well after the stock crash of 1929. But there was no difficulty in their dreams.

In March of 1929, one of the brothers had a sharp dream.

Got the impression regarding the market that we ought to sell everything, including the box stock. Dream concerning my wife and two business associates. A bull seemed to follow my red dress. I tried to catch the bull. Some special reference to Westinghouse and Wright Airplane.

The dreamer, said Cayce, was seeing a "parable" in which the bull represented bullish attitudes about the market among his associates, and their coming attempts, with his, to bolster the market. But, said Cayce, the reference to Westinghouse and Wright as stocks of one of the associates in the dream was a warning to the dreamer to protect the individual accounts in his keeping, just as he might protect his wife from peril. For there would soon be "turmoil as will come by these many changes, as will be seen in a downward movement of a long duration." He urged the dreamer to follow a course of "not allowing, then, those stocks that apparently even are *very* safe, too much latitude," and added that the dreamer's impression "that the body should dispose of all those held—even those in box—would signify the great amount of change as would come."

In more than four years, the dreamer had never received such a dream warning.

In a follow-up reading given the same day, Cayce added that the red of the dress in the dream had indicated the danger in the bull market, and commented that "here is an expected long decline." However, he explained, there would not be "a real bear market" immediately, because "there has been in recent months a much greater tendency for larger combines than there has probably *ever* been before." These would slow the decline. There would also be a major division in financial circles, and—

> *That fight has hardly begun. When this is an issue we may expect a considerable break and bear market, see? This* [*fiscal*] *issue being between those* [*who believe in using*] *the reserves of nations versus of individuals. And it will cause—unless another of the more stable banking conditions come to the relief—a great disturbance in financial circles.*

Cayce was digging out the features of the forthcoming financial collapse, pointing to a decisive battle coming between the representatives of two different monetary policies: those who felt that government agencies should intervene, and those who felt that private financial enterprise could save the day.

In late March, Cayce commented on dream material about Macy's, that Macy's and certain other stocks would reach some peaks, but that there was to be "a long downward movement," given momentum by the proposed government "investigation of banking, Federal, and market speculations." He also urged the two dreaming brothers to dispose of an extra Stock Exchange seat which they held, for "these are near a peak for many days to come."

Just a few weeks later came a strange dream which led Cayce to extended comments on the stock market. The dreamer reported that he had fallen asleep after reading the Book of Ezekiel and "seeking aid from the divine." In the dream he was being blamed for a murder he had not committed; he was in seemingly desperate circumstances, yet he was not too frightened—a fairly accurate picture of how the coming crash would strike him before long. He noted especially the use of hypodermic injections in the dream. Cayce called these precognitive emblems of injections by financiers who would try to bolster the market. He went on:

> *Materially, these are divided between those that would hold the Federal Reserve Board as the criterion for activity, and those who would use the moneys in the various centers for activity as related to the market. As individuals, these are members not so much of the Board—for the Federal Reserve Board is itself divided upon the issue: individuals who have had an ideal as to the functioning of the Board being on the one side, and those that would use the abilities of the Board on the other. And those are fostered—each side—by money powers. But, were these to be allowed to run without check in either direction, there must surely come a break where it would be panic in the money centers—not only of Wall Street's activity, but a closing of the Boards in many centers, and a readjustment of the actual specie and moneys in these centers.*

Cayce and the dreamer were seeing, with prophetic accuracy, the details of the deadly struggle shown in the dream. They were viewing the coming loss of the gold standard, the closing of stock exchanges, and the actual panic that followed in October and November.

In July of 1929, one of the dreamers reported:

> *Voice: "Hold only that which you are able to pay for outright." Saw Fleischman, 82, 83, 82. Big bank failure which precipitated a good deal of trouble on the market. Saw Western Union at 160 . . .*

Cayce assured him that he was getting correct promptings to arm him for coming troubles on the market, including the accurate preview of a bank failure. But if the dreamer could keep listening to his inner voice without fear—and Cayce stressed the importance of acting without fear but in "simplicity of faith"—then he could get all the guidance he needed.

These dreamers and their close associates went safely through the crash on October 29. A few days later Cayce encouraged the chief dreamers of the group to take a vacation. They would, he said, continue to receive definite guidance "in no uncertain manner" on how to act on every major stock decision.

> *Let not the minds be troubled. Let not the bodies become overwearied. Let not the mental become unbalanced by the clamor or the unsettledness as is arising at this time.*

He urged them to take the next few days off, "that they may be able to get within themselves that stillness of purpose as comes from the constant prayer, with those that would aid or guide at this time." Then when they returned to the Stock Exchange, they would find help again, for "those that seek counsel at the Board, at His feet."

The dreamers weathered without severe loss the most trying financial storms of modern times. Their dreams kept them posted on each important stock movement in advance. As Cayce had told one of them five years previously, in first urging him to record his dreams, he was going to be able to see business conditions around him "before the manifestations begin."

Dreams of One's Personal Future

In Cayce's view, it was not only business details which would present themselves in advance to the dreamer. He had told Frances at the start of her dream recording: "any condition ever becoming reality is first dreamed." He meant, of course, major developments that were the outgrowth of the direction and habits of a life—or lifetimes.

He told her this when she was a bride of scarcely a week, dreaming of a weak-minded boy or child. He urged her not to dwell on such thoughts and fears—but the dream was reality for her twenty-five years later, when her only son became a mental case.

Frances also dreamed, early in her marriage, of the breakup that would one day come to her home. But she was not the only one who dreamed of it. On the morning he was to be married, her new husband recorded several dreams. One, which included a voice that warned him to pay close attention, showed him selecting six black veils for his face, at a store. The voice told him that the veils were obstructions to his better understanding and advancement. Cayce confirmed this, indicating that the dreamer was seeing six major ways in which he was going to have to change—either laying aside something or covering something with aid greater than his own—now that he was marrying (and incidentally marrying at a younger age than Cayce had advised him to do, although he was already thirty). On the same night he dreamed that he was back in New York with his bride, who was very serious and asking to be given a chance to adjust to Cayce and her husband's studies of the psychic field. Cayce warned the new husband against overseriousness toward his young bride—a seriousness which later dreams depicted as dogmatism.

A week later the new husband dreamed he and his wife were viewing a beautiful mountain-side, when she suddenly went off to see the other side and left him with a little notebook, where she had written, "This is good-bye." The dreamer was panic-stricken.

Again, Cayce told him he was seeing the peril in his *own* rushing ahead of his wife—giving her more than she would digest, and hurrying on to see the other side of the mountain of his interests. (Later personal involvements ended the marriage.) But there was more to the warning, for the notebook had been a stock-trader's notebook, and Cayce warned both dreamer and wife about their coming temptations to put money, position, and expensive possessions ahead of the real Kingdom of God that they must seek and share.

Marital relations were the subject of the dream of another young husband who divorced his wife some years later:

Saw my father-in-law and myself walking in the court of Park Avenue apartment. Seemed to emphasize the fact that my father-in-law and I were there without our wives. We seemed completely alone, and the actions of mother-in-law and my wife seemed to be equally felt.

As Cayce looked at this dream, he told the dreamer he was short on seeing things from the point of view of his wife and his mother-in-law—qualities that later became critical when the mother-in-law came to live with them.

A man rebuked by relatives for his use of Cayce dreamed that his uncles warned him against a deadly poisonous scorpion. But then the dreamer and a helper drained some fluid from the scorpion that cured the disease of one uncle; everyone rejoiced. This dream, said Cayce, was showing the dreamer a time yet to come when the uncle would need Cayce's aid for a serious ailment, and get it—as he did.

A businessman dreamed of a woman who had been his bitter enemy for years. He was sitting near her in a theater, with tickets that cost more than thirteen dollars, and they were the best of friends. Cayce indicated that the friendship had been broken in the first place because of the actions of a busybody, and that in the thirteenth year of their alienation they would have a chance to reconcile, which the dreamer should take.

Dreams of one's personal future were also about the health and welfare of the dreamer or someone important to him.

Cayce's wife, who often dreamed of the future, and whose dreams were more poetic than most, reported a dream about a relative, which she submitted for a reading by her husband.

I was at her house, with another relative showing me through the house. Especially noticing the white curtains at all the windows, then the going through underground passage—

Here the sleeping Cayce interrupted to say, "Someone to be buried here, you see, soon." She continued: "Of water coming in and me trying to—" He interrupted again to comment that water was, as he had often said in readings, the element from which all life had sprung, and that therefore death was the liberating of the person to the next plane, with the body returning to the first element from which it had come—seen in the flowing of the water. Mrs. Cayce went on: "Of me trying to help get the children to—" And Cayce again interrupted to indicate that the soul was returning to the state of a child, making a fresh beginning in its long journey, by dying. Then Mrs. Cayce finished: "Of seeing a tank of some explosive, and feeling afraid of same." He noted that she was dreaming of the woman's fear of death. But he reminded his wife that in the dream they had escaped the explosive; this depicted the correct attitude toward the coming death: nothing for the woman to fear, for "it is as the Beginning." The woman died three weeks later. She died without the burden of needless anxiety from her close relative, Gertrude Cayce.

Not all of the glimpses into the future by Cayce's dreamers were so solemn. A father-to-be dreamed momentarily while he was praying, and he slipped into a dissociated state. A voice said to him, "Twenty-seventh to ninth." Although it was February, Cayce told him that the voice was giving him guidance on the concern about which he was praying—the welfare of his wife and coming child. The dates in question were March 27 to April 9, during which the baby would be born, safely and happily. Almost two months later, the baby was born right on dream schedule: April 4.

Not a few of the dreams of one's personal future were to be interpreted, according to Cayce, as dreams about one's talents—which for a man often appeared in a feminine form. A dreamer who had developed considerable psychic ability of his own, but was tempted to use it for purely personal advantage, as he was also tempted to use Cayce's readings, reported the following dream:

Someone was paralyzed, by virtue of a stroke of apoplexy. It seemed to be my brother, yet, as I lifted the body to carry it to another place, it changed to a girl or woman—some friend of my mother's. I carried the body about, noticing how stiff the paralyzed side was—also that the head dropped peculiarly over my arm. I tried to readjust this as I engaged in conversation.

In Cayce's view, this dream was a serious warning, to which he devoted two readings. It was a warning to the dreamer that he could lose his own psychic ability, which would dismay him as much as paralysis of his brother or his mother's friend. It was also a warning that when readings were sought for personal gain through the sleeping Edgar Cayce, some of the selfish attitude seeped through and had physical consequences on Cayce's nervous system and circulation. There was no danger to Cayce, this reading explained, in dealing with stocks as part of training a dreamer to dream. But when someone sought stock counsel for dollars alone, under pressure to get ahead of others in the market, it was dangerous for Cayce.

The dream warning was only partly heeded, as later dream warnings showed. As a matter of record, the dreamer lost his own psychic ability within seven years. And Cayce, who two decades later pushed himself to give hundreds of readings to all needy seekers, after his biography was published, died after a stroke and paralysis, paralleling this warning dream.

Finally, there were dreams of one's personal future which only beckoned the dreamer to greater adventures. There were dreams of visitors coming, of an ocean voyage coming, of the coming reincarnation of a friend, of wealth coming, of public acclaim coming. When Cayce and his family were preparing to move from Dayton, Ohio, to Virginia Beach, Virginia, to carry out a long-standing directive from his readings, he was given a series of dreams that showed him the complete hospital which would someday be built there—and was. And he also had a dream about the family turmoil of moving.

Regarding train with Gertrude as the engineer, running into a car, feathers flying, and turkeys in the tool box.

The reading assured him that all things were auspicious for the move; as in previous dreams where food was prominent—the solution to the family's larder problem was symbolized by the turkeys. And the "tools" for daily work would be found as well. Many of the family affairs would seem to be torn to pieces in the move, as was seen in the feathers flying. But Gertrude would provide the necessary driving force for the packing and traveling, and her husband should listen to her—provided she didn't try to "run right over him," as the dream had suggested she might.

Dreams of the Future in Work and Public Affairs

The dreams of the future in daily work submitted to Cayce ran into hundreds. Many were dreams of stock quotations, on scores of stocks and on the companies and industries they represented. Every aspect of a stockbroker's daily affairs turned up in the dreams—including his clerks, bookkeeping, phone calls, customers, competitors, models for success, legal procedures, law suits, leases, partners, and even the time of day for specific sales.

One of Cayce's dreamers was introduced to dreaming of the future at his work with the following scenario:

> *Dreamed a man was trying to sell me a radio. Then someone put poison on the doorknob of my door and urged me to come and touch it. I was terribly frightened. He tried to force me to touch the poisoned knob. Struggling, I awakened in a cold sweat.*

Cayce said the dream was precognitive. There would soon be offered to the dreamer a deal in radio stocks or corporations, represented as "a wonderful proposition." The poison was a graphic representation of the poisonous condition that would follow if the dreamer took the deal. For sixteen to twenty days, Cayce told him, he should stay out of all stocks having to do with radio.

The prospects were more favorable, Cayce said, in the following dream of the same broker:

> *Heard L.M. talking in our apartment, but upon awakening found he hadn't even been in to see us.*

This was very clear and so real I actually thought it occurred even hours after awakening.

In Cayce's view the two business associates had experienced a meeting of minds by telepathy, prior to a deal that would be presented to the dreamer by the other man.

Still a different dream about business associates gave the same dreamer some practical counsel.

Saw a fire escape, which to me meant a way out, and seemed to refer to Pacific Gas and Electric stock we are now long on—own. Horace B. had given me an order to sell his stock, and I had that in mind. The fire escape seemed to be under a great strain, but was steady under the pressure. A man who was long of this Pacific Gas stock, and who is a member of the N.Y. Stock Exchange also, was jumping on the fire escape to test its strength. The fire escape withstood its test.

Cayce assured the dreamer that he was dreaming about that partifular stock, and that his dream was telling him to follow the leads of these men, for his own sales. "That is, when the entity finds these various ones, members of Stock Exchange, are long, be long with them, see? When the sale comes short, be short with same, see?" Then Cayce added, as he often did, that the stock in question would move to the dreamer's advantage one and five-sixths points, very shortly.

The variety of business dreams of the future was striking. There was an accurate preview of the failure of a brokerage firm. A dreamer saw a woman employee leaving him, as she shortly did. One dream had the dreamer looking out over a cemetery while on a bus; it was, said Cayce, a dead stock rising—but "Yellow Cab," not bus stock, which was going up the nine points indicated in the dream.

Cayce himself had an anxiety dream about his own work, when he was out of money, in which his wife hauled him up for trial as mentally incompetent. In the dream he promptly gave life readings for everyone in the courtroom. The reading which he gave on this dream pointed to a specific friend who had appeared in the courtroom scene and indicated that this friend could foster the demand for life readings from Cayce—and thus provide him with the income he needed. It worked out as Cayce dreamed, for he got in touch with the friend, promptly.

But it was not only the work life of dreamers which crowded the stage at night, prompting previews of the future, usually under the management of the dreamer's subconscious. The dreamer could also be shown previews of social service and social action in which he was interested.

Cayce's dreamers were interested in the hospital and university they were trying to build, in order to study his work. Every major development of these institutions was previewed in their dreams. One of their practical problems was finding the right doctor to head the hospital staff; he had to be open to many schools of medicine, yet well-qualified. As it turned out, the one whom they first secured was soon unhappy, as a warning dream of Cayce's showed two years in advance.

> *I thought that I went to New York to talk to the people up there about the institution, and they told me the doctor was already down here, so I came back. Several whom I knew well, and some other people whom I did not know all came with me, and we went down to this place where they said they had the institution. The doctor had Gertrude and my secretary in a great big pot of water boiling them, but it didn't seem to hurt them at all—they were just swimming around in the water without any clothes on. I tried to get them out and burnt my hand. When I woke up, I noticed a red streak or scratch on my hand.*

The reading told Cayce that he would have to work with those in New York to achieve a clear understanding of the duties, abilities and supervision of the physician—or else they would all land in hot water. The scratch on his hand was something he had noted subliminally before falling asleep, and was the same kind of flaw in his body that the plans about the doctor were in his mind.

But not all the dreams of the future hospital were warning dreams. One of Cayce's dreamers saw it in dream a year and a half before it was built, complete with the recreation facilities and sterilizing equipment it eventually contained; he even got the name of one of its first patients.

But the same dreamer also saw in advance the nature of the breakup which one day came among the sponsors of the hospital. This dream occurred a year before the hospital opened.

> *Was going over pictures of various things of Virginia Beach regarding the Hospital. Saw two trains; one was the champion, called the Pankhurst—*

Here Cayce corrected him, by reminding him that the *other* train in the dream had been called the Pankhurst. Then the dreamer continued: "Trains were running to Chicago and New York." Cayce interrupted again, with a note of urgency, and the rest of the dream was not read to him. The dream was on two levels, he said—a feature which he often noted in dreams. At one level it was a stock market dream, showing how rails would be the criterion of coming stock market action, preceding the big crash (which came a year later)—"the general *slump*." He also referred to the national conflict of financial interests coming, in which one side would be the "champion" of truth, and the other a disturbing influence; and he pointed to the need for cooperation between large financial interests in Chicago and New York, as the dreamer had seen.

But then he added that the dream also dealt with another issue. There would come another crisis, when the "pictures" or views of how the hospital should be run would be laid out for everyone to examine. At that time the issue, too, would be whether individuals such as the dreamer would serve as the "champion" of truth and principle—or whether they would bring dissension by the severity of their demands that *others* live up to certain standards.

The hospital closed four years later in a climate of acrimony, where board members challenged each other's living up to principles, and challenged Cayce. Few questioned themselves, nor served as "champion of principle" alone—in the way the dream was urging. Small wonder that Cayce urged the dreamer to go over and over this dream, and recalled it to him in discussing later dreams!

Cayce insisted that to the subconscious, which has the faculty of envisioning the future, time values are not as real as they are to the conscious mind. The subconscious sees things laid out endlessly, just as they are presently headed, until the dreamer uses his will to change them. There are, then, no special symbols set aside to signify the future, for the very idea of future is alien to the subconscious.

Still, Cayce said, there are ways of looking for the future in dreams. One can compare with dream material something about whose future he is consciously concerned—it should come up for comment in dreams.

Further, there are dynamic forces or "spirits" that one can find exemplified in dreams; these are the stuff of which the future was made. For example, the "spirit" of a corporation which wants its stock values high is one "spirit," while the "spirit" of investors who want at times to depress the stock for their own ends is another. Both of these forces need to be studied in dreams of future outcomes. Likewise, in one's personal affairs, there is the "spirit" of his own intentions, and the "spirit" of individuals and institutions with whom he is associated. A good marital or vocational decision ought to be enhanced by a glimpse of both kinds of "spirits" stretching into the future. Cayce used the term "spirit" in this sense to suggest the intent of such terms as "the spirit of '76" or "the Spirit of St. Louis" or "the spirit of a meeting"; he did not mean discarnates.

A different avenue to the future lies in glimpsing the past which has coded the problems of the future. One of Cayce's dreamers, a rebel, was one day going to land in a position where he would himself have to face holding authority. This would be true whether one were computing his future in terms of his having been a rebel in childhood, or a rebel in past lives.

Cayce himself had such a dream which warned him of his future. More than a year before his hospital opened, he saw a vivid scene of a priest being banished, in ancient Egypt. There were throngs gathered in the streets, some crying for the priest's banishment and some for his deliverance, while scourges drove him and his associates before them.

The reading he secured told Cayce he was seeing himself as the priest he had been in ancient Egypt, when marital infidelity had led to his exile, despite the genuine spiritual leadership he had offered his people for a period. Next, ominously, the reading told him that some of the same people who had been involved with him then would bring him similar experiences in this life—"disappointments, fears, railings." When it occurred, he was to do better than he had done in Egypt, by responding with "no malice" nor any other attitude that would hinder his best development as a soul.

Within five years his hospital and university were closed. He was banished to a house overlooking the hospital, where he had to watch it transformed to a night club. He went through agonies inwardly. But he also overcame bitterness as never before in his life, as his dreams showed. The result was that an entirely new group of people, mostly Virginians, now drew around him to replace the New York sponsors of his defunct institutions. And he himself developed, as had been promised to him, new gifts of counsel that enabled him to bring his associates into greater growth than he had ever been able to foster before.

One can look into the future by looking a long ways backwards.

More unlikely than reincarnation to the waking Cayce was numerology. But his readings insisted that numbers were old and familiar emblems to the human psyche, a natural way to dramatize the future. The readings showed his stock dreamers that the numbers in their dreams not only conveyed stock prices, but the days or weeks of stock rises and falls, and the relative strengths of given stocks (a figure of six, for example, was generally weaker than a five). One number or set of numbers might compress all of these indications into one dream image, just as dreams used the face of an individual to convey a variety of associations needed for the dream experience. As might be expected, one of his dreamers was more facile in handling the numbers in his dreams than were the others; in Cayce's view the phenomenon tended to vary with individuals.

Despite the relative indifference of the subconscious to conscious ideas of time and space, Cayce explained, it can pinpoint dates when necessary. For example, a stock movement after Thanksgiving was shown with a restaurant and much holiday eating. A stock development for the spring was accompanied by a glimpse of golfing clothes, to set the time with the opening of the golf season, while another dream offered a glimpse of Atlantic City to indicate that a certain stock action would coincide with the dreamer's trip to the resort city. Yet another dream showed ferries at work to indicate a stock movement after winter ices thawed.

It is noteworthy that where important future developments were coming for the dreamer, these tended to appear in dreams of his close associates or family, as well. Whoever was involved with him, and especially involved without too much ego-concern, would be likely to receive relevant glimpses of the same events. It was as though the future could best be established by the intersection of the dreams of several—as Cayce showed in joint dreams not only on business developments, but on death, pregnancy, birth, illness, marriage, quarrels, and change of position in life.

Dreams of the Unknown Present

Much the same processes work in dreams of the unknown present, according to Cayce, as in dreams of the future. The dreamer's subconscious is using its native ESP, but is moving freely in space instead of time.

One of Cayce's businessmen dreamed of impure milk on the same night that his brother did.

> *We were all out on a party with friends. I fell asleep at the table and we got home very late. My brother got out of the automobile and walked home and left us. First, however, my brother and I stopped to look at a bottle of milk that was marked "Undistilled Milk."*

In the first part of the dream, Cayce told him, he was seeing how partying and late hours were tiring him, as shown in the falling asleep at the party. The solution was to see that these were "left off" until he was rested, just as his brother had "left" in the dream. As for the milk, about which he and his brother had both dreamed, it was adulterated and should be investigated, for the benefit of others as well as of the dreamers. Following the counsel of Cayce and their dreams, the brothers had the milk checked, with the result that the dairy firm was closed by the city Board of Health!

Because of the business interests of Cayce's dreamers, many of their dreams of unknown facts were about stocks. Cayce awake had early doubts that he could supply accurate stock information. So he had a dream of his own. In it he was giving a medical reading, the kind he knew best, and was doing a helpful job. However, he also saw into the body of the lad he described medically, and noted numbers on every bone. They were numbers of stock quotations on the railroad stock which had come up in the first part of the dream. The quotations proved correct, and Cayce was encouraged on the versatility of his readings.

A variety of symbols of unknown stocks appeared in dreams. American Express stock activity was symbolized for one by American Express checks. A subway ride meant subway stock to another. Two autos out of control warned the dreamer about a deal in motor stocks. A row of Pullman cars from different railroad lines, all marked, served to evaluate railroad stocks. A dream of a crowd in an uproar over a lost pair of rubbers was a tip on activity in rubber stock. This little dream took care of two stocks at once:

> *I was drawing lines on the sidewalk. It seemed a combination of Sears Roebuck and Gimbel. Had the impression that it was high enough now.*

Cayce assured the dreamer that both stocks were at their high and should be sold. Then, with his characteristic encouragement for a dreamer doing well, he added information about Wabash Railroad and Missouri Pacific stocks, which the dreamer also held. An accurate dream of Havana Electric being split five for one, before public announcement was made, gave one dreamer "a great deal of money," as he wrote to Cayce. A dream of an obscure stock being pushed by an associate led the same dreamer to inquire of that associate the next day and again to make a killing.

In dozens of dreams, the exact details were given. For

example—slowly and distinctly the following words: "Soo Railway 4% notes at 99 or 100." Here the dreamer was seeing that he should buy these bonds and hold them until they advanced to 99 or 100. The same dreamer, after some three hundred dream readings from Cayce, had a startling dream experience:

> *It seemed I could ask any question about stocks that I chose to ask, and it was answered. I stood under a lighted lamp at about dusk. A man walked up and I asked him how U.S. Steel closed. He said, "It closed crazy, at 178." . . . "Well," I said, "then steel will go on up to around 188 or 190." . . . Then the whole market opened up to me. "Did that man who bought C and O make much money on the purchase?" "Not much," came the reply. The leather stocks seemed indicated for something, particularly Endicott Johnson. Then the others that I can't remember—all, everything I wanted, seemed to flow right to me or into my consciousness. Even as I awakened I seemed to be asking about Fleischman stock, and even after I awakened the voice said, "Use your own judgment on Fleischman."*

In addition to the factual promptings in the dream, said Cayce, it contained a full promise that the dreamer could have guidance on every stock he desired, if he could keep his life and purposes straight. He had been through an experience of attunement like Cayce's dream of the mounting spiral. It is not surprising that this dreamer became a millionaire in the space of months.

A secret business deal was depicted in a dream as a fraternity having an initiation. An office boy trying to steal stocks was shown in a vision, but with a warning that he should be treated gently—helped to see that such temptations come to everyone. A poorly planned business deal was depicted as a defective baby. A dream of bandits looting travelers on a train was, said Cayce, a warning to an inventor that someone was trying to steal his new product. But a competitor seen lighting a fire under a table was only cause for care, as the dreamer should note that the fire never reached the table top. A dream of a holdup by a chauffeur led to Cayce's counsel that the man be released from employment. Cayce's own dream of a hog and peacock helped him to see how those who hogged the show in his work were of as little value as those who strutted much and did nothing.

But the dreams showered facts about personal affairs, just as freely as about workaday life.

A father was tipped off that his small daughter's nursemaid was playing scary games with her, by a dream about a frightening beetle in his daughter's bed. A young woman seeing her boyfriend in a compromising situation with another girl was warned she had dreamed the facts correctly. A college student dreaming he was debating was shown his relationship with every one of his close associates, by the way they functioned in the dream. A woman who dreamed of her relatives discussing medical care for her invalid mother saw the essential life quality of each relative laid bare in the dream. A businessman was led by a dream to new friendships with two respected attorneys who shared his psychic interests but had never mentioned them.

What occupied the dreamer awake occupied him at night, as well, but with new facts added by dreams.

CHAPTER X. DREAMS OF THE LIVING DEAD

In the outlook of the Edgar Cayce readings, death is a transition for the soul as a birth is a transition. But it is not an extermination.

How Cayce himself came to view death could be seen in a dream of his own. The dream, which came during a reading, presented its viewpoint with the charm and grace which were hallmarks of Cayce's own consciousness at its best.

I was preparing to give a reading. As I went out [of consciousness], I realized that I had contacted

Death—as a personality, as an individual, or as a being.

Realizing this, I remarked to Death, "You are not as ordinarily pictured, with a black mask or hood, or as a skeleton, or like Father Time with a sickle. Instead, you are fair, rosy-cheeked, robust, and have a pair of shears or scissors."

I had to look twice at his feet or limbs, or even at the body, to see it take shape.

He replied, "Yes. Death is not what many seem to think. It is not the horrible thing that is so often pictured. Just a change. Just a visit. The shears or scissors indeed are the most representative implements to man of life and death. They indeed unite by dividing, and divide by uniting. The cord does not, as usually thought, extend from the center [of the body], but is broken from the head, the forehead—that soft portion you see pulsate in the infant.

"Hence we see old people, unbeknownst to themselves, gain strength from Youth by kissing there, and Youth gains wisdom from Age by such kisses. Indeed, the vibrations may be raised to such an extent as to rekindle or connect the cord [there], even as the Master did for the son of the widow of Nain. For He took him not by the hand—which was bound to the body as the custom of the day—but rather stroked him on the head, and the body took of Life Itself. So you see, the silver cord may be broken, but vibration . . ."

Here the experience ended.

A man in his mid-thirties, whose late father had been a strong influence in his life, dreamed his way through the death barrier in an unforgettable sequence. The dream began with girls, who were important in his life and dream symbols, and then moved to bed, where he had last seen his father dying:

Now I beheld a vision of many beautiful women, all dressed in different colors—but they were not women after all, but lights, beautifully colored lights, which I interpreted as Spirit entities. They appeared before me in line. There seemed to be one particular shining light that I knew was my father.

Cayce confirmed that the dreamer had entered the "Border Plane."

Then my brother said, "Why don't you turn out the lights?", meaning the electric lights in our room. This I did, and behold, my father appeared in bed with me. Now I was at the head, he at the foot of the bed, but although I seemed to recognize his physical form, yet it was not as I had previously seen him—instead in this same manner of a man, Light, the color of which was like the sun.

The light, Cayce said, represented the directing force from the dreamer's own superconscious realm; like an altar light, it could be trusted in what it showed him.

I burst out crying, and wept bitterly at my father's nearness. The light flickered a bit, and many things flashed through my mind all at once. As this: it didn't do any good to cry—it didn't help my father; and why didn't I talk to him, instead of crying.

I said to him, "I love you." The light flickered again, and I thought, "Maybe he cannot understand words," so I put my hands to my lips and childlike blew him a kiss. Motioning, with my lips whispering, "I love you." Then the light took the shape of my father's head, and out of his mouth came the words, "I love you, too, Son!"

The light came nearer to me—up towards my end of the bed, and unwrapped a package; on the inside of the paper wrapper I beheld my father's handwriting. I could distinguish the signature as my father wrote it, and although I could not make out any of the contents written, I recognized the handwriting.

At this my emotions very nearly again overcame me—I was very close to my father indeed.

Cayce confirmed that the dreamer had entered into the "fourth dimension" of existence, beyond death, where his father would help him understand how things were, as the next portion indicated.

Then the box inside the package came to my view, and being opened by my father, revealed four Chiclets—chewing gum pieces. "Take one," my father said. I did, and it tasted very good, and as I chewed he told me to take another. I did. There were still two left.

Here, in this homely sequence, the dreamer was being shown, Cayce said, that he would have to chew and digest fourth-dimensional existence for himself, through such dream experiences, for he could never reason it out correctly otherwise.

"Follow me," said my father. And I saw the light upon the wall. It was flat like a mirror reflection, yet not perfectly round as I first thought, but had shape. I cannot now in my conscious moments recall the symmetry of that light on the wall, but I do wish I could. It had shape, but how shall I describe it? What shape was it? I remained in bed, regarding the light, my father's spirit.

Then the dreamer heard a voice address him by name, a voice he had heard before as the call from his own superconscious being, or best self.

"Follow your father." I got out of bed and followed the light. It traveled along the wall, sometimes leaving, taking shape in the air—from room to room, finally into the kitchen. Then I lost track of the light. I

was left in darkness, seeking my father, seeking his spirit-light.

The dreamer would have to learn the truths about life beyond death little by little, Cayce said, emptying himself of "self." But then discovery would come, for "seek and ye shall find." The dream continued:

I was then returning from some party—it seemed I was coming from the lawn of a fine estate. My brother and his wife and others were at the party. I was still seeking the spirit-light of my father and his guidance. Above all, I had in mind what had been given in my wife's dream, that my father would reveal fourth-dimension life to me. I sought that, as I yet do, above all.

Here the dreamer betrayed his fascination with the question of life after death—a fascination which would later bring dream rebukes and urgings that he keep a well-rounded life and pilgrimage. But at the moment something more immediate came into view.

Then I emptied the contents of a bottle of whiskey I was carrying from the party, and I smelled the alcoholic fumes. The Voice: "Not in such an atmosphere will you ever find your father." Again I was in the dark room seeking my father's spirit-light.

In this incident, Cayce commented, the dreamer was experiencing for himself how his heavy drinking deadened his psychic perception, and how his heavy partying took his creative energies in another direction from the seeking in the dream. He needed to look for something better to give others than the momentary stimulus of social affairs—as the next portion showed him:

But something happened then. Behold I was naked, and able to fly in graceful fashion through the air. Others, too, seemed able. First, I watched the others, gracefully traveling about, here, there, everywhere.

"They are really spirit entities," I thought, "and their flights represent their universal energy; but my physical mind must see them as men, otherwise it can't understand." One of these men dropped upon his head, and got right up and gracefully flew again. "See," said the Voice, "not a sensuous being. He didn't hurt himself at all." Then I tried and started to fly. It was wonderful, gracefully floating through the air. But I had work to do, some purpose to perform, as had the others.

In the dream, as so often stressed in the Cayce readings, contact with the dead had as its first purpose a transformation and quickening of the dreamer.

I descended through the roof of a house to find men committing a burglary. "Oh," I cried at them, "Life up here is so wonderful—so much is in store for you! What you are doing is not worthwhile!" Then, pointing my finger at them from my position on a ladder, I said: "Thou shalt not steal. Thou shalt not commit murder, thou shalt not commit adultery, thou shalt not commit fornication, thou shalt not bear false witness, thou shalt love thy neighbor as thyself."

They cried, "Hypocrite!" at me. "You have done these," they cried, and chased me out of the house. I ran panic-stricken to another house, where I found a gun, and hiding behind a table awaited their arrival. Someone entered, and I shot at him repeatedly. It was my friend who had died recently who entered. Approaching me, dressed in his tuxedo, he laughed as he said, "Here, try another shot—hit me here."

Now, Cayce said, the dreamer could see how a life not well lived brought fear that blinded him to the realities of life both before and after the grave. Such fear would make a man blindly shoot at a dead man. But the dreamer must shoot, as his friend was laughingly showing in the dream. However, he must "aim"—concentrate the energy of his whole life—toward worthy goals, not toward destroying others in panic. Apparently the dreamer got the point, even in the dream, as the next scene showed him in a different mood:

> *My friend in the tuxedo and I sat down to a table and he told me a funny story, at which we both laughed heartily.*

The joke, Cayce said, was how ridiculous so many human actions—like shooting at a ghost—seemed when viewed from the perspective of eternity. It was time for the dreamer to laugh a bit. For it was necessary, Cayce added, that "laughter, gladness, be the message of each entity in every manner—not the long-faced fellow that gets his way, see?"

The journey into the realms of death had led far. It had led right back to the dreamer's daily life. And the last sequence placed it there firmly.

> *Again I felt my father's presence—didn't see as before—but felt it. I was still seeking. The Voice: "Chicago Milwaukee, 69—75."*

A very practical quotation on a railroad stock. It came, Cayce said, to show the dreamer that creativity in work life was not of a different order than the creativity which governed exploring through death. The laws of stock movements were ultimately the same in origin as spiritual law, physical law, moral law. It was all to be found from the same Source and Giver. Not from discarnates, but from the Lord of life, Himself.

It was an affirmation that the Cayce readings never failed to make.

Dreams for the Sake of the Dead

Contrary to what the living may think, according to Cayce, not a few of the dreams where the living meet the dead are for the sake of the dead.

Sometimes the dead simply want to be known and recognized as still existent. The dreamer who reported the vivid experience of his father, above, had already dreamed a meeting with his dead grandmother. The dream began, as many such dreams of contact beyond the grave, with a note of beauty.

> *We were in a room together, many of us enjoying ourselves and planning and trying to accomplish something. I heard beautiful music, and the rest seemed to vanish, and there lying before me on a trunk, which was in the room, was my grandmother, my mother's mother, who had died one day before my father. Happily I kneeled beside her. I could only see her face and neck, and I put my arms about her neck. She seemed to be crying, or not exactly crying, but greatly distressed. She said "None of you want me to live." "How can you say such a thing, Grandma?", I answered, and attempted to kiss her. But she grew more distressed. "Your mother doesn't want, or care if I live," she said. I put my arms about her closer and tried to explain that Mother certainly did, but just didn't understand. The vision ended there.*

Cayce confirmed that this had been an authentic contact, and warned again, as he had already told the dreamer, that to seek contact too often with a discarnate would bring distress to the discarnate, holding the dead back from their own full journey. Yet he added that there was also distress brought to them "by not understanding, by not hearing, the call"—just as the dreamer had seen.

Still more distressing was the dream of a young man about his father-in-law, who had recently taken his own life. In the dream a voice commented, "he is the most uncomfortable fellow in the world," and then the dreamer was shown his own baby crying for food. The image was to convey the dead man's hunger for guidance and spiritual sustenance, said Cayce. The next night the dreamer heard the man's own voice, together with "a wandering impression of restlessness." The voice said, "I seek rest. I want to leave and be with my family down there." Again Cayce said the dream contact had been authentic, showing the dreamer how much his prayers were needed for the father-in-law—who was still an "earthbound" discarnate. He added that the reason the discarnate was turning towards people in earthly life was that "the lessons *are learned from* that plane, see?" It was a point Cayce often made, that souls who had once entered the earth had to learn their final lessons in the earth, where will is called into play in a fashion different from existence on other planes.

Yet contact between the dead and the living can be joyous. Sometimes it occurs because the dead want to show the living what death is like, to take away their fear and grief. Exploring the possible reality of such contact, one dreamer had her side pinched by a discarnate friend, so vividly that she screamed in fright, while another had his toe pulled when he asked for it—and did not ask again. One dream took a man inside the brain of a woman dying of cancer, a relative, and showed him precisely what a relief death was, when it finally came. A later dream also showed him how a soul feels when awakening to consciousness after death and discovering he is with his body underground—and then bursting up through the dirt towards the light.

The startling fact, Cayce said, which all these dream experiences were making clear to the dreamers, is that the death-state is more nearly a normal one for a soul than is earthly existence. The usual human question of whether earthly consciousness survives death is backwards. The important question for a soul is how much of its normal awareness and creativity, and contact with the divine, will survive its birth into a body.

The fact of the normalcy of the death-state explains why Cayce, on entering his trance for readings—a trance much like a pre-death coma—was given the suggestion that "Now the body is assuming its normal forces," so that he could find and give the information needed for the reading. But life on earth, in this view, is also valuable. There are insights for the soul into creation and the Creator, which can be gained on earth as nowhere else. These are insights that "angels," whom Cayce described as beings that have not undertaken earth incarnation, will never know.

Discarnates are not only rewarded by recognition from the living, or even by the joy of teaching the living. They can also, in relatively unusual cases, work directly with the living for the fulfillment of worthy causes.

Because certain well-developed souls see more after death than do the living (except in the dreams of the living), these discarnates are in a position to bring to the dreamer guidance on many things: health, financial affairs, social causes, social service, relationships with the living. But they pay a price to do it, Cayce insisted, and warned that the dreamer who finds such aid has special responsiblities to stretch his own talents to the absolute maximum, while wide awake.

Cayce himself had sometimes received aid from discarnates. Such an experience occurred spontaneously some months before the opening of the hospital, when what seemed to be his dead mother spoke through Cayce at the start of a reading for someone else. Cayce remembered the contact later as a dream, but the others in the room heard the words spoken aloud. His mother, who called him "Brother," seemed to be talking to him about a fountain which Cayce had planned as a memorial to his mother at the entrance to the hospital. She felt he should let his sisters help, as well as his father who was still living (but not for long, as she correctly noted). The sleeping Cayce spoke with animation: "Mother!" Then he repeated her words aloud:

> *"Mother is here. And you haven't written Sister yet, and told her—Sister wouldn't like it, Brother, and she'll feel hurt! Write to Sister, tell her, and Sarah and Ola and Mary—they'll all want to have a part, and they'll feel just as you do. And after a while when everything is straightened out, it will be so nice for you all to know that Mother will be right with you! Be a good boy. Write, Brother! Talk to Mother. Be good to Papa. He will be home before long. But write to Sister—and tell the children Mother loves them all."*

Cayce did write, and the fountain was built as a joint effort. It was, of course, one of the harder things to lose when the hospital was later given back to its Depression-struck founders.

Meeting his mother was not Cayce's only experience of being guided from beyond death on how to raise money for his work. Years later, when he needed a fireproof vault to be built onto his modest home, as a safe place to house the records of his readings, he had an experience which he reported to friends as follows:

On the evening of November 4th, I had this dream, vision, or experience.

I was in our office "reading room," discussing with some of the family the necessity for protecting and preserving the records we already have, and the means for doing this. Suddenly a "master" (the *Master, to me) appeared and said:* "Peace *be unto you! Ask all whom you have tried to help to* help *you save these records, for they are their experiences and are a part of* them*! Whether they contribute a shingle, a beam, a window, a door, or the entire vault for the records, give them all the opportunity to have a part in the work."*

Cayce wrote to everyone who had ever had a reading recorded, and explained how they might contribute. Two years later the fireproof vault was dedicated—paid up.

Neither the dream of his mother nor of Christ seemed to Cayce experiences limited to him. He insisted to the dreamers he coached that wherever people were prayerfully engaged in some project of service, they would draw help from beyond the grave.

When one dreamer had seemed to secure dream aid for months on stocks, through the assistance of his discarnate father, so that he could amass funds to support the Cayce Hospital and Atlantic University, he had the following charming dream:

My father in some way indicating something regarding a cigar I was smoking.

The father had been devoted to cigars, and Cayce commented on the "joy, satisfaction, contentment" seen in the dream, as father and son discussed the aroma of good cigars. It was an indication, Cayce said, of the good feeling in which the father and other discarnates were working cooperatively with the son—teamwork from both sides of the grave to accomplish a humanitarian work.

Dreams of Telling Others About the Living Dead

In later months the father appeared to assemble a team of discarnate financial experts, who aided the dreamer with promptings while asleep and awake. Cayce took this development as factual; he made his contribution by coaching the dreamer to keep a level head in the strange partnership. But the dreamer's relatives were skeptical and hostile, however wealthy his efforts were making him and his associates. Stinging with their rebukes, he had the following dream:

It seemed I traveled to a place by boat, and there beheld the Master—Christ Jesus.

I shouted to all about me as loud as I could: "We can be like Him—I have proved it! We can be like Him—I have proved it!" None would listen or believe me.

I entered what seemed to be a grocery store, and there beheld a man who appeared as Christ—it may or may not have been He, but he was dressed as Christ would have been, but younger. A woman said to me, "Isn't He a wonderful God?" "You can be like Him," I answered her. "Oh," she replied, "you are not like Him. You are a soft, mushy human."

I turned to show her Christ, and it may have been His picture on a box I showed her. But there He was, as I knew Him from pictures I had seen—an older Man, sympathetic, yet unyielding in His faith in the Truth, and its adherence, and propagation to His fellowman.

I went up to the store counter and sat down. There behind the counter I saw the younger man, like

Christ, kneeling down in prayer. He was thanking His Father for much.

I leaned my head in my hands and cried bitterly. "It hurts in here," I said, pointing to my heart, and it seemed this referred to my inability to make others understand—and also that He suffered just this way.

I said: "What is the use of the real, the true, if we are ridiculous to all here on earth?"—and I saw myself as ridiculously crying my message, "We can be as He—I have proved it." Then I saw Him again, kneeling down in thankful prayer, and crying, I said, "It hurts to my very soul."

Then the voice—it may have been His Voice —spoke and said, "They shall return again to earth to learn. They shall kneel down and worship. . . ."

It was a dream which mirrored the center of the Cayce message, as an experience for the dreamer: "We can be as He." Cayce often referred back to the crucial phrase of this dream.

But the dream also contained deadly peril of inflated self-importance for the dreamer, as later dreams showed. And Cayce interpreted it guardedly, commenting only at the end of his reading that the dream could be seen as a message from Christ. The dreamer had, he said, almost entered into "the Holy of Holies, gaining strength and wisdom from Him who *is* strength and wisdom." He might through his dream begin to understand the cry of Christ on viewing the ancient capital city of Palestine: "O, Jerusalem, Jerusalem! How oft would I have gathered thee together, even as a hen gathereth her brood under her wings, and ye would not!" There was then but one course for someone determined to carry a difficult message to his fellows: to be "oft in prayer," for "those who seek Him, the Master, may find Him" as well as "strength and endurance in body, soul and mind."

In some ways the hardest lesson for Cayce to pound into his dreamers, when they became convinced of the reality of life beyond the grave, and of shared work with discarnates, was that they should not try to prove their view to others by psychic feats. No such proof should be attempted, he warned them over and over. People could be invited to explore for themselves, but demonstrations were out, exhortations were out. Exactly as Jesus had taught, no "sign" was to be given. Men's minds and hearts were to be won another way, by the quality of life shared with them.

The same issue lay in telling others about Cayce, as he commented on a later dream where he referred back to "I have proven it," in his interpretation. The dreamer reported:

> *I entered a room where there were many people and saw a man asleep—lying there asleep. It may have been Edgar Cayce.*
>
> *I was worried about Pan Petroleum stocks, and the oil. Many were looking to me for advice at the same time. Then I said, "Oh, well, I can't converse with a sleeping man as easily as if (the way it is with my father) I could talk to him even though not a word is spoken—where I get my advice, from guide."*

He was bragging in the dream about his stock and other counsel from his discarnate father, coming to him "direct" instead of through the sleeping Cayce. He also showed some scorn of the very people he was supposed to be helping: "Seems the others didn't ask the understanding to get that advice."

But then the dream changed swiftly, to reach through to his better motives:

> *Then a little boy dressed in rags entered. I felt sorry for him, and putting my hand on his head, said, "I'll take you in and love you." Then a man who seemed to be the child's father came in and the boy pointed him out to me. I said to him: "I want to take your son and care for him." Then the man answered: "I can support him and bring him up, if I had my health." Then he showed me a paralyzed arm. I felt terribly sorry, and thought I would like to use my power (of communicating with my guide) to convert the man, again*

with the sleeping man—and then talk with these people and explain in language they would understand what they could do.

Then I saw the sleeping man in what appeared to be a department store window, and crowds of people there, looking through the glass window at this phenomenon.

As Cayce discussed the dream, he said the sleeping man represented both Cayce giving readings—in a state where mental and cosmic and spiritual forces were all combined to be helpful—*and* the sleep of onlookers themselves, where they might "through dream reach mental, spiritual, cosmic forces" that could be carefully correlated with waking experience to "gain knowledge through which the mental, the material, the moral, the *whole* being of man may be benefited, see?"

He was turning the dreamer's attention away from his dream feats to the question of what others could learn to do in their dreams.

But how were others to become interested? The dream dramatized two ways in which one might try to reach others.

One was the way represented by the man sleeping in the store window. This appealed to only a part of the mind of onlookers, not to their capacity for perfect understanding. It catered to the element of "mystery," to the "moment's understanding," to the sense of the "extravagant."

The other way lay in the episode of the child and the father, where the dreamer felt the prompting to compassion and helpfulness. It was the way of "education or knowledge for the young; assistance to those halt, maimed or in distress physically or mentally" which might far better "bring them in relation to those Universal Forces, in relation to God" through dreams and awake.

Besides, people who needed to understand life after death would find it in their own dreams, if they looked.

Among Cayce's dreamers, a dead husband came in dream to assist his widow to reclaim the estate from a crooked administrator. A mother-in-law spoke from the dead to warn a dreamer against poor companions. A father who had served as a dreamer's guide threatened to drop all assistance from the next plane if the son played around with women any longer. A dreamer who reported wrestling playfully with a dead uncle in a dream was told by Cayce he had slipped unknowingly in his dream into "the Borderland," where he and the uncle had enjoyed a happy time together.

Dreams came to Cayce's subjects to show them the kind of vehicle or body they might have after death, how they would know they were dead, how they would progress through various planes, and what sort of helpers they would find. Much was unfolded in their dreams about communication with the dead: how their perception was one sense seeming to be several, how they mustered energy for contacts with the living, how they gathered to listen where the living taught about death, how they longed to speak through a psychic, how some who were poorly developed would try to take over a living person left open to their influence by his attitudes or actions or poor health.

Question: When Is One Ready For Dreams Of The Living Dead?

In commenting on hundreds of such dreams, Cayce offered a number of answers.

First of all, one is ready for such dreams when he has them. His subconscious will not feed him experiences he can't handle if he chooses to do so. Secondly, one is ready for dream contact with the dead when he will not speak lightly of them. In Cayce's view, such dreams could mean dangerous escapism.

Thirdly, one is ready for dreams of the dead when he soundly loves and serves the living; such dreams always come for a personal reason, a personal growth of the dreamer, or some concrete service in the regular round of his daily life. Dream messages seeming to come for a general public are immediately suspect, for healthy contact with the dead was not designed to function for the living in this way.

Fourthly, one is ready for dreams of the dead when he is

as ready to give aid to the dead as to receive it. When prayer for a discarnate comes freely and naturally to mind, then visions of them may follow. Any other approach tends to be exploitative. Fifthly, one is ready for dreams of dead loved ones when he has worked through his griefs and guilts regarding them, and has forgiven them for hurts to himself. Lack of this makes a nearly impenetrable barrier.

Finally, one may dream of the dead when his own full life draws to its natural close, and it is time for him to prepare for the next journey.

Dreaming of Reincarnation

One of the "dead" who will live, said Cayce, is the dreamer himself. In dreams he may meet himself as he has been in other lives.

There are two ways in which such dreams might occur. One, a relatively uncommon mode, is that of recalling a scene from a past life exactly as it once happened. The other is dreaming of a present scene, but with the plot supplied by forces from a past life.

In Cayce's view, one does not simply leave past lives behind; one lives all of them in the present, in some degree, and at varying times in the life. Consequently, dreams often carry forward the action of the past personality as it is called into play by events of the present life. Such dreams show the dreamer and his associates in modern dress, as Cayce explicitly indicated, but re-enact "karma," or the heritage of past-life themes and traumas and talents, just as other dreams re-enact similar motifs from childhood in this life—and still other dreams combine both.

Such a view made it difficult for Cayce's dreamer to distinguish dreams rooted in the present life from those which also had past-life roots. To Cayce this distinction was not particularly important. What matters, in his view, is that the dreamer act on the dream. Whether from one life or a dozen, selfishness must still be conquered, talent risked, love given and refused and given again. Unlike many fascinated by the idea of reincarnation, the sleeping Cayce brought it up only when it might specifically help a dreamer to understand himself or someone else. Otherwise, he stuck to the present choices before a dreamer.

But there were hints that all serious dreams may be read as embodying some degree of past-life themes. The life of the soul is woven of these many threads, however modern the present design.

When Cayce himself dreamed that a woman friend of his was used as a gunshield by bandits, whereupon he shot the leading gunman and rescued her, he was told by the reading that he should act as the woman's "protector, teacher, guide, director" in their present relationship, because of an association in a past life. The fact that all were in modern dress in the dream only accentuated the need for "modern defense" of her "activity, thought, or purpose." When he dreamed that he and one of his sons quarreled and the son left home, he was told that he was seeing the kind of stress they had known together in a time of Egyptian history, and that both he and his son would have to watch temper and tongue.

A woman who had in another lifetime controlled men with her beauty dreamed of competing with attractive women, to hold her husband in this one. A woman who had in another existence led her people as a female warrior was having in this lifetime to learn to control her power drives or alienate all who came close to her. A man who in a previous life had doubted the religious mission of his brother kept dreaming of his present brother turning on him. A young man who had been a king in another life was warned about his airs as a Southern gentleman in this life. A bright woman who had been the daughter of a philosopher dreamed of how to make her tongue yield to her heart. A man who in a past existence had used his power for the exile of a leader dreamed constantly of how it felt to be rejected by those in power and influence. A professional man who had been a rake in a life not too far past dreamed repeatedly of being caught and humiliated while making love to a woman not his wife. A woman who had been an actress dreamed of the choice between being a real artist and a show-off. A man who had used military power to humble others found himself belittled in his dreams by military figures.

At least this is how Edgar Cayce saw their dream plots

and tangles. How could the dreamers achieve a perspective on such claims? By dreaming actual memories from past lives, he told them.

And dream they did. They dreamed of words, names, phrases in ancient Hebrew and Egyptian and Persian tongues. They dreamed of vivid foreign scenes: an oasis, a huge man in Arabian dress bending over the dreamer and threatening his life, tents of the Israelites encamped near Jerusalem on their return from Babylon, rays and machines from the ancient civilization of Atlantis, fishing on Galilee at the time of Jesus, the ceremonial dedication by thousands of a pyramid in Egypt, death by combat in a Greek arena, the landing of ships in early America, the conflicts of Israelites with Moabites, the Roman rule of Mediterranean countries, the spread of Hindu thought outside of India, and the moral force of ancient Chinese teachings.

Typically such dreams were not mere scenarios in the night, but episodes vividly focused on a present problem of the dreamer.

When Edgar Cayce was under stress amid the quarreling of backers of his hospital, shortly before it was closed and sold, he dreamed the following during a reading:

> *I thought I was with Mr. and Mrs. Lot and their two daughters running out of Sodom, when it was raining fire and brimstone. What had been called "she turned to a pillar of salt," because she looked back, was that they really passed through the heat—as came from the fire from heaven—and all were tried by that. I got through the fire.*

To his surprise, Cayce was told by his own reading source that he had been there with Lot, as someone sent to warn of what was coming. He had actually accompanied the family in their frightening experience, which was reviewed for him now because he would have to pass through another kind of "fire" himself, in suffering with his associates. Whether he would again escape would depend on his "attitudes and activities." To prepare, he should study the life of each individual reported in the Bible story.

A practical Jewish businessman, weighing what to make of the figure of Christ, dreamed a startling vision:

I fear to write—or as I write this I am still frightened from this vision. But it must have had its import in my life, and it is that which I seek.

I visioned something pertaining to the Lord Almighty dying, and then something happened just one and a half years later.

What happened, and how does it pertain to my present life?

The death of the Lord and this subsequent happening one and one half years later reminded me of the death of the nineteen-year-old king, Tut-ankh-amen. What relationship does the Lord's death, and a following event (what was this event?) have to the death of the nineteen-year-old pharaoh?

In responding to this dream, Cayce told the dreamer, as he often told those who dreamed materials which he felt were out of past lives, that he could solve the riddle of this dream himself by turning his mind introspectively. One did not have to be asleep to get in touch with such memories.

The dreamer had once been very close to Jesus, even in his household, and experienced the immense shock of his death. He was only a young man then, and it took him a year and a half to make up his mind to acknowledge the place of Jesus as his "Master." It happened when he was just nineteen. He had been "a deep thinker" then, and a student of ancient cultures, on whom the helpful rule of the young Tut-ankh-amen had made a strong impression, especially the way he had knit together divided households. The young man of Palestine at nineteen had identified with the young monarch, and when the traumatic events and choices of his Palestinian lifetime came flooding back to him today, so did the associations with Egypt that were in his thoughts then. Now he was in a family divided by quarrels over the meaning of Christ for Jews, and he would have to look beyond surface appearance and loyalties for the deeper realities that applied. This was why his dream had taken him back through the centuries.

Cayce told those whom he coached on dreams that the study of reincarnation was just as important as the study of life after death. He put it to one woman this way: "For, if individuals were as mindful of what they have been as they are of what they are to be, this would become a much more interesting as well as a purposeful experience; for then, as He gave, those being on guard do not allow their houses, their own selves or their mental abilities, to be broken up."

PART IV. SELF-DEVELOPMENT THROUGH DREAMS

CHAPTER XI. THROUGH DREAMS TO A HEALTHY BODY

Although Cayce emphasized the power of "mind the builder" to shape each person's life, he insisted that the body be reckoned with in every stage of growth. As he saw individual development, the mind is cradled snugly within the body, and deeply affected by endocrine gland function, as well as indirectly affected by diet, exercise, eliminations, posture, and other considerations. With this view Cayce took a position near to that of modern psychiatry.

Historically, he took a position about the role of the body in human growth which set him nearer to Judaism and the Bible than to Greek and Gnostic thought, which had alternated between worship of the human form and treatment of the body as a prison of the spirit. Cayce once commented in a reading that the body, for a human being, is as natural and intimate a structure for the soul as a fingernail is for a finger.

In this perspective, dreams of course deal with concerns of physical health. To be sure, Cayce pointed out, many dreams deal with physical health and other concerns at the same time.

An associate who was slow in raising money for the Cayce Hospital dreamed that he was constipated. Cayce interpreted his dream to refer both to physical constipation, which needed attention, and to constipation of his money-raising, which was halted by the dreamer's holding back too much of the initiative for himself. Another dreamer saw himself falling in the wet snow of a street, where he lost his gloves and lost track of his brother. He was seeing, said Cayce, that he needed to prevent undue winter exposure, and he was also seeing that he ought to follow his brother's counsel more closely, both in health matters and in matters of business.

A businessman dreamed vividly of a relative who was just then leaving the hospital after major surgery.

> *We were all out to the farmhouse, and she was coming home from the doctor, coming home alone. As she came in the room, I hid behind the door, so that she wouldn't see me. She was very pale and trembly, and was uttering something about another operation. Someone in the crowd said she was nearly hysterical.*

This dream, said Cayce, was a serious warning to the relative to slow down during her postoperative period. The dream had been set in a farmhouse because it was "all feeling," as distinguished from a dream about mental activities. The dreamer had been shown hiding, because the dream was about a hidden complication developing, which would necessitate a second operation if the woman were not careful. And she herself was shown "trembly and hysterical" to indicate the warning, as well as her inward hope of recovery without repeating the pain of her first surgery—pain which would not be necessary, with care.

The warning was given serious attention, unlike some of the health warnings that came to the same dreamer. His wife opposed his use of osteopathy. This explained, said Cayce, his dream of going to meet somebody in a secluded hotel. The dream was indicating that he should get the care, even if he had to keep others from knowing about it!

Quite different was the dream of a woman soon to become pregnant:

> *I was going in to swim from a rickety platform, very unsubstantial in its structure. As I jumped in, or tried to dive in, I made a belly-whapper—i.e., landed on my stomach. It hurt.*

The entering into the water, a variation on Mother Sea or the mother of animal life in evolution, was here, he reported, a symbol of her preparing to enter into motherhood. But her body was not in shape, for it required physiotherapy and exercise to rearrange and strengthen some organs; thus the "rickety platform." She ought to get busy with the requisite medical care, for "this greatest of offices given to the sex—woman."

As often occurred to the dreamers being coached by Cayce, her second dream of the same night dealt also with the same question.

Was back at college, and was going to room at the dormitory. I wanted two rooms to live with two other girls, and I wanted my own private bath. I wanted good meals. Decided not to stay because the food was poor.

Here the dream showed her need to prepare for the coming pregnancy—both physically, as shown by emblems of food and bath, and mentally, as shown by her desire for space and privacy in the dream.

Her husband had vastly different dream material about the body:

I beheld a great advertisement in electric lights, shining out on Broadway. It said: "The substance of matter and mind is one and the same thing."

Cayce said, "This truth, and the understanding of same, should be emblazoned on the minds and hearts of people," as the lights had signified, over the "thoroughfare" of life.

In Cayce's view, matter and mind are two of the three original orders of creation (which he said are "matter, mind, and force"), and while different, each comes from and answers to the same Creator. For him there was never ground for dualism which disparaged matter.

The dreamer continued the report of his dream, which was typical of the philosophical or reflective type that appeared scores of times in the Cayce dream records.

Then I added that the difference between matter and animal is that matter is a materialized-changed form of this one substance, whereas animal is this one substance organized to become materially manifested as mind.

The dreamer's view was much like Cayce's. For Cayce saw all subhuman creation moving slowly towards consciousness, with the mineral and vegetable and animal kingdoms successively ruling the earth in that order, and needing human consciousness to crown the progression. The dreamer went on with his dream:

That the difference between animal and man is that the animal organization's development is confined to the section of the process of the one substance that becomes changed into a materialized form. Whereas the organization of man-mind includes in the materialized form a development gained in all the other sections of the process of this one substance.

The dream was correct, Cayce said. Animal consciousness is limited to what develops out of its life span, whereas human consciousness, because of the role of the soul, also includes elements from vastly different realms of creation. Man is made to contain within himself all the patterns and modes of creativity yet devised by the Eternal (there could one day be more), for man's is "the highest created Creative Energy in the material plane."

Then Cayce spoke about death, where the separation of orders of creation becomes clear. At death "that of the material kingdom remains material. That of the spiritual kingdom remains spiritual. *Man* develops the soul, in that experience (or lifetime) along *its* plane of existence. Like the animal, the human body (at death) becomes as dust to dust. Like the body of the beast, all dust to dust moves in its accumulated forces, going on *its* . . . phase of the development, see? While the spirit force goes on in *its* own sphere, see? Yet all of One Source, for we are brothers all." In Cayce's view, material creation has its own laws and destiny, just as the soul has its own laws and destiny. Souls now in earth lives have become disoriented, and too often try to live the way of the soul by the way of the animal—not an unworthy way, but wrong for them, in the appointed plan of creation. Reincarnation is a way of learning about animals, bodies, earthly creation, while still following the long destiny of the soul.

In a beautiful dream allegory of his own, Cayce saw the process dramatized. He saw himself living and dying in existences as various animals, alternating with incarnations as a human being. He was a snail, a fish, a cow, a dog, a bird. He was also a fisherman, a herdsman, a military guard, an Indian, and a Civil War soldier. His reading on this dream specifically told him that it was *not* literal, but emblematic—although touches of his real past lives as a human could be found woven into the fantasy. What he was seeing was what a human can learn of animal creation, from fear of extermination to mother love, with hate of other species and finally service of others—all symbolized in the animals of the dream. He was also seeing the greatness of human existence and companionship, yet how it was distorted by confusion with learnings from the animal kingdom.

Cayce's readings held unfailingly that men never incarnate in nonhuman bodies. But this dream had taken Cayce inside of animal existence in the most poignant way, to show him what humans learn in earthly lives about the manifestations of the One Force in its various orders of creation. All else but souls is appointed to endlessly disintegrate and reintegrate; souls, like their Maker whose eternal image they bear, are to endure.

Dreaming of the body's concerns takes many forms.

Dreams of Body Function

Cayce's dreamers submitted to him dream materials that touched each major system of the body.

There were dreams of circulation. A man dreamed that a rash broke out when he cut himself shaving, and Cayce said he was seeing evidence of poisons in his blood, which needed iron. When he dreamed later of gland trouble in the throat, he was, said Cayce, seeing endocrine malfunction, due to anemia. When he dreamed that his tonsils were removed, he was being warned of a different type of circulatory congestion. Another dreamer reported a dream in which eating refreshments at a family party led to hot words and a fist fight; he was seeing, according to Cayce, that some forms of alcohol were good for him in moderation, as in the party scene, but not the alcohol produced in the blood by too much sweets—which had dominated the party scene just before the fight.

There were gastrointestinal dreams. Cayce himself dreamed of a little wheel in his head that had stopped turning because of needing oil. The reading said he was seeing how his headaches derived from an intestinal need of lubrication to counteract constipation. A dreamer reported having a woman doctor treat a sore toe for him while in a store where many were eating ice cream and sodas. The helpful woman represented, as often in a man's dream, an element of guidance—in this case away from a sore point (Cayce said, "in common slang, a 'sore toe' to the entity"), which was the dreamer's overindulgence in sweets.

There were respiratory dreams. The impact of a cold was shown to a dreamer as sailors washed overboard into the sea. A bronchial infection was shown by choking. There were dreams of hypochondria, of sexual malfunction, of impaired metabolism, of nervous disorders.

Dreams of Bodily Care

When a dreamer reported how his legs had ached in a dream of a long train ride, Cayce pushed him to more exercise. When the dreamer reported seeing his brother paralyzed in a dream, Cayce said it had partly to do with danger to the brother's health, but mostly with the dreamer's own tendency to go stale, from lack of rest and play.

There were dreams of changes in diet. A man dreamed that tomatoes would be good for his wife—and Cayce concurred. Another saw himself brought a demitasse when he ordered a large cup of coffee; his subconscious was showing his taking too much caffeine for his nervous system, said Cayce. A dream of codliver oil led to dreamer's taking it, while another dream urged him not to bother his wife sexually while she was menstruating. A series of golf dreams sent one dreamer golfing, while another's dream that a trolley ran over his raincoat led him to dress better out-of-doors. As a result of dreams, a mother took better precautions to keep her baby from falling, and changed her habits to place him in the sunlight more.

Cayce had a vivid dream of being in church as the service was about to begin, when the floor suddenly caved in. His reading told him to avoid the "service" of others through his readings until his body was in better general shape for the strain. He took a vacation, for he and his family well remembered those frightening few times when his trance had turned to a coma from which he would not awaken, despite all the suggestions given him.

Dreams of Medical Care

More than a few dreams evaluated particular doctors, sometimes with approbation and sometimes with disapproval that led to a change of physician. Others evaluated the effect of particular drugs on the dreamer. Once Cayce himself dreamed a complete eight-part pharmacist's prescription for treating his cold—and found it helped. There were specific dream warnings of how to avoid danger from diptheria and polio epidemics. There were dreams counseling sweat baths and fasting.

And of course there were dreams of the element of prayer as it could participate in healing. One woman dreamed of two doctors, but could only recall the name of one. Cayce reminded her that the other in the dream had been the "Great Physician," whose aid was much needed along with medical care for her dying mother. When a man sought to understand in a dream why his prayers for the healing of another had not been effective, he dreamed that "two plus two equals four" as part of the dream. Cayce explained that in such healing "there are two consciousnesses to be made manifest with the one psychic or spiritual law"; doubt and fear in the mind of either one could block the function of a law otherwise as real as mathematics.

Question: How May Dreams Of The Body Best Be Used?

Cayce never encouraged his dreamers to be their own physicians. He saw most of their dreams of the body as sensitizing them to concerns which they already had, but were neglecting. Or he saw such dreams as prompting them to consult their physicians.

He did not urge them to take dreams of death and severe

illness as literal—for often, the subconscious might dramatize in such shocking imagery only tendencies that could in the long run lead to medical trouble. In thosc few cases where actual death was at hand, he pointed out that dream material often dealt less with bodily concerns than with psychological and emotional concerns, preparing the dreamer and others to handle the coming transition.

He noted the frequency of some dream element of actual body function when dreams are about the body. Food, or medicine, or pain, or a part of the body is set in focus, or a doctor or nurse is at hand. Bodily dreams are not obscurely symbolized. Nor are they isolated: if the warning is important, they are repeated, and not infrequently given to relatives, as well.

But the body may also appear emblematically in dreams, Cayce said. Feet can be one's stance or foundation; pain can stand for suffering. In the case of one dreamer, kinks in his hair were kinks in his reasoning.

A few of Cayce's dreamers had repeated dreams of animals, which he said dramatized both bodily function and—more significantly—psychological attitudes which such animals symbolized. To help them understand these symbols, he set some of his dreamers studying the imagery of mythology, and even of the Book of the Revelation in the Bible. He developed for them an entire theory of the function of endocrine glands, in response to psychological factors. It was a strange aspect of his interpretation of dreams and symbols, but to the sleeping Cayce all as matter of fact as a sore throat, a miscarriage, or the benefits of swimming for a sedentary financier.

CHAPTER XII. ORIENTING THE LIFE THROUGH DREAMS

In the view of Cayce's readings, no man can or should invent his own life.

There are too many unknowns for consciousness to grasp. There are the impulses, talents, and problems from one's past lives. There are currents of social, political, and religious change moving beneath the surface of one's times, which require unforeseen responses from an individual. There are souls waiting to be born as one's children or grandchildren, if certain choices are made. There is a spark of the divine in every stranger, needing to be found and fanned into flame. There are discarnates clustered about men of good will and hard work, some waiting to learn and some waiting to help. There are even angels to be entertained unawares.

Given all these unknowns, no man can be expected to invent the best trajectory for his life—for his vocation, his marriage, his community, his causes, his people.

But it is enough for any man to begin with the best he knows.

Souls are not judged by absolute standards, Cayce said. They are judged by their fidelity to their own ideals, their own understanding. And they are not judged by their failures so much as by their willingness to get up and try again.

It is better, he often said, for an individual to be doing something with his life, even if it is wrong, than nothing at all—just drifting. For when a life is put in motion on the basis of the best one knows, however inadequate the vision, helpful forces are always called into play, both within and without the individual, which can straighten his course into an adventure of growth.

One does not need to invent his existence. He has only to "use what is in hand" and "the next will be supplied." For there are two helping forces always at work, to guide the unfolding and spending of a human life.

One force is a person's own original spark of creative energy, a force placed in him at creation, and bearing a potential for love and creativity as great as that of the Creator Itself. The other is a spirit "abroad in the universe" of helpfulness, of unending creativity, kindness, and wisdom, which was for Cayce typified by Christ, because He so fully exemplified it as a soul. This other force will "seek its own" within the individual when allowed to do so, and magnify whatever is good within the person.

In Cayce's view, dreams are of prime importance for the meeting of the ultimate creative force of a person with that other force which ever seeks to help him.

A stockbroker who was wrestling with the question of what God wants with human souls dreamed a bold and unforgettable vision, where God Himself came to his apartment. The dream began by focusing on the dreamer's daily work.

> *I was in what seemed to be a railroad station and purchased a lot of candy. I paid $1 for each box, and anticipated selling them for $2 apiece.*

The dreamer was seeing, said Cayce, his own vocation of buying and selling stocks, which often seemed to him luxuries like candy amid the world's needs, but were in fact necessities. He had told the dreamer before that God was God of "the Street" as much as of temple or hospital. The dream continued by highlighting the dreamer's desire to serve others:

> *While carrying the candy out to the automobile, I saw a woman with children, also laden down with bundles. I felt I should like to help her with hers. "If I just could finish this work—get these out to the car, I'd help you," I said. "Oh, that is all right," she replied. "We have a car outside, and it isn't so hard or far." I noticed that she was well-dressed, had an automobile, and was burdened with what seemed radio batteries—particularly the child was carrying such.*

He was seeing his desire to be of more help than his present round allowed. But her affirmation that she could help herself was a reminder to him that his best service would always be to help others to find the best in themselves. Part of this he could do by being a very good stockbroker. Then in time he would also be able to teach and write, sending forth "messages" that were symbolized by the hint of radio. He had to walk the road of duty in his daily life, and would find this led to the promise of companionship with the divine, offered to every soul as its destiny. This was the burden of the next part of the dream.

> *I returned to my work. It seemed menial, not pleasant. It was necessary to work, and although I seemed reduced in position and the kind of work, I remembered "the promise"* [given in earlier dream] *that I should be "risen unto Him," and found happiness in that promise. I started to sing as I worked, carrying the boxes out.*

As if to underscore this thought, the dream now swung to practical stock counsel, where the dreamer saw a business associate doing something ridiculous at the Stock Exchange.

> *I was seated in a room upstairs with Wm. L. He seemed to be playing a musical instrument. Then he asked me if I bought any Hupmobile stock.*

The dreamer should note, said Cayce, that the incongruity of the scene was already a warning to the dreamer about that particular stock.

> *"No," I replied. "I don't want any of that." "Then you won't be in on the move we are in."*

> *I saw loads of Hupmobile stock sell, reams of it coming out on the tape, thousands of shares at the time. Hup is selling at around 21-22.*

Again, said Cayce, the element of incongruity was a warning about this stock, although it would soon be very active, as the dream suggested. The warning was further emphasized by the dreamer's inability to place his order.

I rushed to buy 100 shares of stock, but couldn't get the order in. I reached for the stock exchange phone to put the order in myself, to buy 100 shares of Hupmobile stock at market, when L's order clerk took the phone from my hands, as though to say, "This isn't your affair." He said to me, "I'll put the order in for you," and he did so. Then I went back and sat down with L and noticed he started to play the guitar, or banjo.

Clearly, Cayce commented, the dreamer was being warned not to act on this stock at present. Instead, he should study it, using his conscious judgment. When the prospects looked good later, from a conscious viewpoint, then he could turn to the subconscious for confirmation, and "that as is necessary for the use as regarding same will be presented at that time."

Was the dreamer to check on such stocks only in dreams, or also while awake? Cayce said the next portion of the dream showed that he could have guidance both ways, if he worked at it:

Then I was at home—our old living room, it seemed, in our Uptown home.

The setting of the old home and its associations was meant to indicate, Cayce observed, both the good values associated with home life there and the possibility of conscious guidance from the dreamer's now-dead father. The dreamer was already sensing that he could, by focusing his life on his highest values, and by the time and care spent in attunement, begin to call forth more guidance through telepathy than he had yet known—as the next part of the dream showed, with its hint of attunement across distance:

The radio was going, and my mother and brother and I were enjoying it, the first two dancing to its tunes—I seated listening. Then it seemed we could not get any distance. I tried to tune in, and could not. I wrapped some wires around a spool, and attached this instrument to the machine, seeking thus to perfect and tune in, but it didn't work. Yet it should have, could have, might have. I gave it up, and we resumed listening to local stations.

The dreamer should on no account give up, Cayce insisted. Help was available.

Then our maid came in and said, "You should be close to the front door, for God may come in. He will enter that way." My brother and mother paid little attention to her, but I perked up at once and started forward.

The maid was shown doing the announcing, said Cayce, because "he who would be master must be the servant of all," and "a little child shall lead them."

Then the maid announced the distinguished visitor, that "God" was calling on us. I rushed out into the hall towards the door. Half way to the door I met God, and jumped for Him, throwing my arms around His neck, and hugging him. He embraced me.

The resemblance to the story of the Prodigal Son rested on the dreamer's deep regard for his own father, who had appeared in other dreams as his first glimmer of "the Heavenly Father."

After that, I noticed God's appearance. He was a tall, well-built man, clean cut and clean shaven, wearing a brown suit and carrying a gray derby hat. He had an intelligent look, an eye that was kindly but piercing. He had an expression that was firm and features clean cut. He was very healthy, robust, business-like and thorough, yet kindly, just, and sincere. Nothing slouchy, shuffling, maudlin, sentimental about Him—a man we might say we'd like to do business with. He was God in the flesh of today—a business or industrial man, not a clergyman, not dressed in black, not a weakling—a strong, healthy, intelligent Man, whom I recognized as the Man of to-

day. And whom I welcomed and was glad to see, and recognized in this fine upright Man—not the ordinary—but God.

There had come to the dreamer, Cayce affirmed, a "vision as has been given of old, as even appeared to Father Abraham in the day of the destruction of the cities in the plains." The dream had shown God as a man, not as a servant but as "an equal in every way and manner—appearance, conversation, in dress" in order to burn into the dreamer's consciousness the realization that God desires to "make man, when man presents self in the fullness of self, equal *with* that Fullness. As has been given, 'We will make man in our own Image' " by "giving man that portion of the creation" within man's very soul, whose impulse would be "that man may become as God and One with Him."

It was a daring dream picture of the intent of creation itself, where man's destiny is to become an equal co-creator with the divine, and yet not the Whole. The pattern was not so strange, said Cayce, for it had been shown "even as the Son of Man in flesh appeared in the world, and made Himself one with man—yet His will, His force, His supply (drawn not from Himself) coming from the All-Powerful Force."

There is nothing automatic about the promise, Cayce affirmed. Each person must choose to put aside whatever blinds him, whatever distracts him—"that as is preventing man in the present from recognizing the force, power, manifestation, of the God that is presenting Self to man in everyday walks of life." The problem can be seen in the next sequence, set in Prohibition days.

Then we passed my liquor closet—it was half open. God looked in; I showed Him the half-opened closet. But, I thought, I forget He is not the ordinary man he looks, but God and knows all. So I might as well show Him all, as pretend anything.

It was a response not out of keeping with repentance.

So I opened the closet wide for Him to see. I showed Him my liquor, particularly the gin which I used for cocktails. "In case of sickness," I said to God. "You are well prepared," God replied sarcastically.

But it is not only lawbreaking, deception, indulgence, narcotism which shut man off from the divine, Cayce pointed out. The dream itself now turned to the deeper problem of "lack of thought, lack of quiet introspection," leading man to miss "the great love that is shown" and "the great force and power as is manifested," and "the great good as may be seen" shining right through and transforming "even those weaknesses, or that as is considered as of sin."

We proceeded into the parlor, where the radio was still playing, and my brother and Ma amusing themselves with it. I wanted them to meet God, but they couldn't seem to recognize Him.

"Of course they would not know Him," I thought. How could they recognize Him, when they have not the faith that He did appear in the flesh long ago in Christ, and that He could, might, may appear in the flesh again in just such a Man as was before me. If they don't understand how God appeared in the flesh Christ, how would they recognize a flesh God today?

How could they understand that the true manifestation of the true perfection within us constituted the manifestation of God—whether of a man in one capacity or Another? So they did not see, or at least pay any attention to Him.

This portion of the dream called forth urgent response from Cayce, who said that each individual must "know that when they are in tune with the Infinite, how great must be that power which is set in motion, to bring about the manifestations of the divine that is within them"—with this purpose: "that men, others, thy brothers, may know that God *is*, and is the Rewarder of those who diligently seek Him." Such aid is not won by merit, nor found by abdicating selfhood. "Not as a gift that is bought, not as something that would take the place of the individual self. But as the natural consequence of the love of the Father for his creatures, for His Self in the soul, His portion in man, that would be One with Him."

God's aid to man, said Cayce, is not a vague, abstract assistance, but as concrete and immediate as the daily work or daily prayer, which the next dream scene showed. For this was He of Whom it was said, "Not one sparrow falls to the ground but what note is taken of same."

I sat down on the sofa to converse with Him. "You could work harder," He said. I almost started to reply, yet bethought me that God knew all—no use. I meekly assented. "You could hardly do less," He continued.

"How did you make out in Hup Motors?" he asked. I couldn't just say—not so well, it seemed. "That is L's purchase, L's recommendation, isn't it?" asked God. I knew that God knew before the asking. "Yes," I replied. "About all you have been doing lately is lifting capital, isn't it?" said God, motioning with his thumb towards my mother (from whom I had just borrowed). "Just about," I assented.

God looked toward the radio. I was standing, studying the radio, as God disappeared.

The dreamer was being shown, said Cayce, "in that simple way and manner" where he must begin. As the radio made possible transmission from one human being to another "the things, the conditions, the good, the bad, that is taking place in one, how much more—through the infinite forces—must the cry, the pleading, of every individual come up to the Father on High!"

It was time, Cayce noted, for the dreamer to "take stock of self" in the light of this vision, to examine himself as a "servant of the One"—but as a servant who too often "sees not, because of the blinded eyes of self." Yet he should not despair, but attune himself as the radio suggested, "for the promise is to the faithful who do the biddings of Him, Who is the Giver of all good and perfect gifts." Stocks were His to give, but much more. He could bring an entire life to bloom, "for in Him we live and move and have our being."

The weight of such a dream not surprisingly tempted the dreamer to look down on others who had not received such dreams. Accordingly, he had another vision to correct his outlook. It was simple, but direct:

I turned in bed, and beheld before me a statue in marble. It appeared as standing right next to me, or next to the bed right in the room. It was a headless statue, such as are represented in marble of the Greek God, Zeus. As usual, I became frightened (it was so vivid), but I felt assured when I reasoned that the statue was but an image or reflection of those lights that I now beheld on the ceiling. "Only an image of those lights," I reassured myself. But the statue remained, and so did the lights.

Cayce confirmed the dreamer's sense that the statue and the lights were connected, for he had seen a representation of spiritual force and material results, of the lights that bring forth men's products and creations. Each man, Cayce reminded the dreamer, is ultimately building his statue of the divine with the best he knows, whatever name he gives it, or no name. That he might not know the source of the One force is shown by the statue being headless. But each does what he can to bring into form what he believes is the "All-Powerful" in the universe, and no man can properly measure or condemn this effort in his brother.

Each individual must instead wrestle with his own evil, with those temptations which can hurt him and others. These are not so difficult to find, Cayce told the dreamer, "for as has been well given, three conditions prevent man in earthly plane from visualizing the spiritual elements in all phenomenized form in the physical world: pride of the eye, weakness of flesh, desire for fame." Each of these produce fear and doubt in the individual, making him lose his perspective, as the dreamer was shown in a startling vision:

I was anywhere at any given time. I was contemplating the wonder of the inner power of all phenomena of the Lord.

I was reflecting upon this power's direction of forms away from the One Self—hypnotizing its portion, as Bergson puts it, so as to appear in individual flesh form, and material phenomena.

Also saw my life experiences in this form, and I was very happy in my double vision of the outer form and the inner process.

Then a girl, seemingly representing the wisdom and consciousness of this inner power, and who seemed perfectly aware of my limited knowledge, threw a stone into space. It passed like a shooting star through the skies, and hit some animal there in space.

"He is going to get something he doesn't expect," said the girl, referring to me. And behold, it was so, for the stone, striking the animal in space, brought it to earth. There were two of them, and they were in cages. On earth they crawled along on their belly like a hideous snake, yet with head and neck upraised like powerful dragons. They moved around, dragging their cages with them.

Elsewhere Cayce described dragons as the sum of human passions and animal energies, as he discussed the symbology of the Book of Revelation.

They came close to the girl, close to other things: and although they looked dangerous, and I feared greatly for everything and everyone the animals came near, they seemed to do no harm—in fact helped matters. How, I cannot say, for I felt them a menace—i.e., viewed them with fear, but observed they did no harm.

The fear was in me, the hideous interpretation of what I recognized in me. But good seemed to be in them, for they suddenly changed from hideous animals to pretty little children, freely laughing, and dancing in glee.

Then, said the dreamer, the same point was made in a different way:

I was in a house with this girl who seemed to represent the power, the inner impetus, the Lord of creation—or as this power was represented in me, my subconscious self, which in a lower dimension is also present in all things.

I was in the material house, and knew my elusive pretty companion was also there. Yet I had much to learn about her, and she determined to give me a lesson. Mind, now, I knew she was there, saw in the vision the lesson she planned to surprise me with —that is, I was supposedly unaware of her plans.

I climbed the stairs of the house, and as I did so, the girl said to someone, "We'll give him a surprise and teach him." This all behind my back, so to speak. As I entered the room, instead of the beautiful girl I expected to find, I beheld a hideous black face, so ugly and so ferocious that I fainted with fright! Upon awakening, I beheld the figure transformed again into the pretty girl. She stood over me, winsome, smiling, and encouraging. Happy—recognizing the spirit of her—I was yet afraid.

The dreamer himself guessed that the dream had shown him how fear distorts human experiences, human energies. Cayce told him he was correct, and that fear and selfishness are prominent in what men call hell, for "they are what first separates an entity from God." The girl, as often in his dreams, was the force of truth in his life, teaching him.

Human passions may be monsters or playful, hideous or winsome, depending entirely on what human beings do with them. In themselves they are only power or energy. Cayce pointed out this theme in many of the dreams submitted to him.

Dreams of Passions

There were many dreams of sex in the hundreds submitted to Cayce, employing varied emblems. A dreamer interested in an illicit love affair saw himself as chasing a shiny white pig. In another dream he saw himself falling through trapdoors and caught in a maze of wires around his legs—traps and entanglements, according to the Cayce reading. One dreamer more than once saw himself playing a game where spikes were placed in grooves. Another dreamed of himself in a morass with his secretary trying to pull him out; when she couldn't make it, she said, "Then pull me down." It was a dream not difficult for Cayce to interpret. But Cayce did not devalue sexual energies, instead constantly urged his dreamers to live well-rounded lives. A woman who withheld herself from her husband was admonished to think the problem through for herself, not to call upon his readings to justify her.

Anger, too, has its proper place in human affairs, as Cayce interpreted dreams of hostility. One can, as Paul had said in the New Testament, "be angry but sin not." However, anger mixed with cruelty, fear, and defensiveness has its own way of poisoning the angry one, not only mentally but even physically. A dreamer who found himself in a dream as a general, mercilessly slaying the enemy, was seeing, said Cayce, his own vengefulness which so often led him to dream of being persecuted by the Ku Klux Klan.

The peril of selfish fixation was underlined, said Cayce, in the dream of a man too proud of his ancestry and clan; he clung to his wife desperately while an "elevated" train swayed dangerously on its tracks.

Part of the answer to the call of passions, in Cayce's view, is play and playfulness. One must take time to do many of the very things shown in dreams—go to the theater, converse with friends, read, golf, take trips, read the comics—whatever one knows from experience worked best for him.

Dreams of Success Strivings

One of Cayce's dreamers had a memorable dream experience of Christ. But in the dream, Palm Beach proved stronger than Christ, for the dreamer lost track of Him as he name-dropped before wealthy associates in a resort hotel. The dream warning was not one which Cayce had to labor. The same dreamer saw himself in another dream as coming to two bridges, a higher and a lower, and taking the lower, even though he had to crawl to traverse it, because it was more familiar to him. Cayce said the dream had set before him a choice of two ways of life.

But the choice that faced his dreamers was not between asceticism and tasteful surroundings. Cayce found nothing the matter with wealth and position, provided they weren't the ultimate goal. When a dreamer saw himself rebuked for having damaged the front of someone's fashionable New York brownstone, he was told by Cayce that his ideas were indeed going to embarrass some of his fashionable associates. But the damage would not be permanent, to him or to them, if he stuck by the truth, for "God is God, even of the brownstone house."

The lure of wealth came not only to others in dreams, but to Edgar Cayce himself. More than once he saw himself as eloping with a lovely girl, leaving his family behind. In addition to sex drives, his readings told him, he was seeing his own temptation to put wealth ahead of prior commitments. Nor did he escape dreams of illicit drives to fame, through lecturing to women's clubs, or locating treasures, or even contacting the dead. He would make his place in history, his readings assured him, but not by such performances—instead by the quality of his service to others.

A dreamer who was slight of build and emotional of temperament longed to be famous before his fellows, as his dreams kept showing him. The way of pomp was dramatized when he saw himself an officious ship's captain. A different and better way showed a boy named Tom doing creative things with radio antennae throughout an entire town. Showing people the way to attunement in their ordinary lives was a better service than being captain of an ocean liner.

The lure of psychic ability was often in the dreams of those who turned to Cayce, because of his example and their own experiences under his coaching. But the lure brought with it warnings. One man saw himself responsible for bringing Cayce out of trance, but leaving him there in grave personal danger, in order not to offend party guests with the strange sight of a hypnotized man. He would have to choose, said Cayce, between love of appearances and developing real ability.

Equally compelling to Cayce's dreamers was the call of wisdom, stimulated as they were by the range of knowledge on which Cayce drew. One man dreamed of knowledge as a dog which turned and bit him. Others dreamed of truth as a beautiful woman, coming down the stairs or even standing at a bar—but capable of appearing ugly, and of making imperious demands. Cayce himself dreamed of wisdom as a snake, after losing the hospital had cured him of some airs. In the dream the snake spoke to him, saying it would not harm him further, after he had chased it with a large stick—the "rod or staff of life" given to those who are faithful to God, said the reading of the dream.

It was difficult for Cayce to train those with newly found dream powers to place them in a balanced life. One man dreamed that he was getting help in his golf game from a discarnate who told him he couldn't help him if he hurried so much. The next day, after contemplating the dream, he played the best game of golf in his life. The same question had to be faced in business and in home life, said Cayce, as well as in psychic development.

Dreams of Serving Others

A man given to many words found himself stirred in a dream, as he often was, to match wisdom with service. He saw a small child whom he wanted to take for a canoe ride. But the way was blocked by one event after another. He was seeing, said Cayce, the impossibility of service without devotion to the Source; without that, things had a way of never working out, however admirable the intentions.

A businessman dreamed that his brother was bored while he discussed his own hobby. It was, said Cayce, a reminder that if one wanted the interest of others, he had to be interested in them. Indeed, the ultimate worth of everything the dreamer said and did for others would be unconsciously weighed by others against the quality of his responsiveness to them in the little things of life.

A dreamer given to fantasies of his solitary grandeur as he pursued spiritual things was the subject of a dream where he saw chorus girls kicking in step. Unless he could learn to work with others at least as well as they could, said Cayce, his development would not go far. It was the same thought in a different setting which prompted Cayce to dream of a study group while he was giving a reading for them. He saw the face of Christ, and noticed how it changed as each member of the group was given a message in the reading. By reviewing those expressions, Cayce was told, he could help each member of the group to learn something about his own willingness or unwillingness to cooperate with the others in the studies before them.

The old tensions between Christian and Jew were often to the fore in dream material submitted to Cayce by his Jewish dreamers. One of them saw a resolution which Cayce commended. He was in a swanky dress shop which was running out of dresses, and told the proprietor he knew where to get the needed dresses "wholesale," from an East Side shop of lower status that carried excellent merchandise. The shops, said Cayce, were the Christian and Jewish establishments, respectively, and they needed to form a partnership because of what each could give the other.

But the changes that must occur to bring man closer to his full stature, in modern civilization, would not be accomplished primarily by the heads of religions or the heads of state. When a wealthy man dreamed of losing his job and his social status because of a book he was writing, Cayce told him to go right on with the book and the ideas it represented. In seeing himself poor, he was seeing that whoever would really serve must be "all things to all men." Moreover, he was seeing something else he intuitively understood, that what is "termed the mediocre class of individuals in the physical world bear the brunt of the whole nations, as a people"; so, from the ordinary folk "must come that balm, that leaven, that will leaven the whole lump." The key to lasting social change was helping ordinary people to help themselves.

All real service to others begins at home, Cayce told his dreamers. When a man dreamed that his pregnant wife had triplets, Cayce told him he was seeing that one and one make three—not only in the way two parents produce an offspring, but in the way husband and wife complement each other in many ways, and produce more good than the sum of their individual talents.

But family affairs were not absolutes. When a man saw his mother's face slapped in a dream, he was told he was sacrificing her well-being to the appearance of family harmony.

In Cayce's view, the service of others is central to human destiny. But it is subject to as much distortion of motive as are passion and success. In his view, service and attunement go hand in hand. Service without attunement leads to manipulation of others—doing good that never works out. But attunement without service leads to inflation of the dreamer and to his eventual paralysis, for "to know and not to do is sin."

Dreams of a Free Life

In Edgar Cayce's readings there is the promise of a way of life that offers a free and joyous spirit in the midst of the laws and contingencies that govern human existence.

Cayce himself reported that he had lost this sense of joyful freedom for many years, and then—after suffering and rededication—suddenly recovered it.

> *While meditating in afternoon, the same exuberant feeling came over me that used to years ago, but which had been lost to me for twenty-five years.*

When he submitted this experience for a reading, he was told he had been through "an experience of the inner self awakening to those potential forces as may become the more active . . . in those of the meditations." From this time on, Cayce gave silent meditation a larger place in his life, and urged it more often for those whom he trained.

The same reading added spontaneously, "As has been given, there shall be in the latter days, 'Your young men shall dream dreams, your old men shall see visions, your maidens shall prophesy.' These are coming to pass, with the upheavals as are just before the world [1932] in many a quarter!"

One of his dreamers reported a similar experience, after working on dreams for over a year.

> *While reading James'* Varieties of Religious Experience. *I submit this, as I can't tell whether it is a religious experience of my own, or whether it was purely a case of nerves, i.e., physical or pathological.*

Cayce interrupted him to say, "An *experience*—not nerves." Then the man reported:

> *While reading, a sudden quivering came over me. I felt every pulsation of my heart, of the nerves, of the blood. I became conscious of a vibratory force moving everything within my body—even the chair upon which I was sitting seemed to be in motion. I was not asleep—*

Again Cayce interrupted, and the report was not finished. He told the man he had experienced the physical effect of the "consecration of self, self's impulses, self's inner self" to the manifestation of the One Force in his life. He had undergone an authentic spiritual experience. In fact, Cayce added, it was an experience that could be traced "through the various ages of man's development," and he offered these illustrations:

> *Swedenborg, as he studied.*
>
> *Socrates, as he meditated.*
>
> *Paul, the apostle, as he meditated upon the happenings of the hour, with his inward purpose meeting that spiritual force in man which brought his self-conviction; the entity, then, being over-shadowed by the Force as seen, see?*
>
> *And as was by Buddha, in that position when meditation in the forest brought to the consciousness*

of the entity the At-Oneness of all force *manifested through physical aspect in a material world.*

Cayce told the dreamer that in his moment of quickening he had seen and experienced the kind of personal baptism meant in the Bible—"My Spirit beareth witness with thy spirit, whether ye be the sons of God or not." This joy, this trembling sense of spiritual reality at work in human life, had been no deception. But it was meant to have concrete fruits. For Cayce told the man that from now on he would not only receive greater insights into the human lot, but he would have to counsel more people spontaneously seeking his aid regarding their daily lives. His prediction proved accurate.

Such lifting up would give a man a new sense of freedom. "But love is law and law is love," Cayce told him. The freedom came to put him in bondage—to those who needed him. Not painful bondage, not sad bondage, but grateful bondage.

Many months later, Cayce referred back to this experience while reading James, when the dreamer reported dreaming that his little baby was not afraid. This dream showed exactly the right outcome of such experiences, said Cayce. "Except as ye become as little children, ye shall in no wise enter in." Such attunement could genuinely cleanse and renew a man, even when he had made drastic mistakes, until his spirit was as fresh as a child's.

The same dreamer had made a costly error of stock judgment, one which cost him and his associates thousands of dollars. It was the last he ever made of such magnitude, for he learned from it to better follow his inner guidance. But he berated himself for it, as seen in a little dream fragment which contained only two words "My fault." Commenting on this fragment, Cayce insisted that one should never be afraid of errors honestly made, if one's purposes were sound. One could and should walk free of self-condemnation, for such self-destroying was never intended for man.

A harassed businessman reported this dream, early in his work with Cayce:

A man approached many, including myself, in what seemed to be a hotel lobby. When he first approached us, he had the appearance of a detective, but as he drew near I had the feeling that he was Jesus Christ.

This little dream, said Cayce, had caught the whole force of God's ways with man on earth. He would be found coming to each person as Man to man, coming from out of the crowd in the hotel lobby. He would be as ordinary as the next face seen but capable of changing each individual, each group, even the masses and crowds, if taken seriously in one life at a time. His ways might seem restrictive at first, but they were not. He came to set men free. The dreamer, too, could walk among his fellows in this same manner and purpose, if only he would choose.

In Cayce's view, the dreams which come to a seeking man can unfold to him the very structures of creation, itself, if he needs to understand these. He interpreted dreams which he said were about destiny, about the One Force, about evil, about the outer void, about Mother Sea and the Heavenly Father, about laws, about grace, about the soul and its voyage in the ship of the psyche. These matters are important, for they lead to understanding and conviction that can reach to the farthest depths of the mind and heart.

But orienting the life through dreams means beginning much closer than these far vistas.

Such a beginning was enacted in one of Cayce's own dreams—a quaint dream, but pungent, that came when his hospital and university were being closed, and when a number of dreams offered him encouragement.

About an old horse that in real life had died twenty years ago.

It was climbing up a hill. We turned it loose so it could pull itself up, and we walked behind it in the tracks the horse made. I said it was a good thing the horse had just been shod, so that the feet would make tracks for us to step or climb by.

The reading on this dream interpreted the horse, as Cayce's readings often did, as the bearer of a spiritual message. Cayce awake might feel his message was spent, and his life of little account. But he should take one step at a time.

Then, if he looked, he would find that where he stepped there were tracks to walk in. There would be places made not only by new horseshoes, but by the Messenger Himself—Who goes before every man to lead him, "sure of step, but constantly mounting."

Out of imagery as plain as the memory of an old horse, his dream had fashioned for him a promise.

It was a promise fulfilled, for his best readings and most helpful training of others were yet to come.

It was a dream where the eternal was hidden in the ordinary. This was the promise Edgar Cayce's readings perceived in all dreaming, for all dreamers, in the century which had rediscovered dreams.

THE A.R.E. TODAY

The Association for Research and Enlightenment, Inc., is a non-profit, open membership organization committed to spiritual growth, holistic healing, psychical research and its spiritual dimensions; and more specifically, to making practical use of the psychic readings of the late Edgar Cayce. Through nationwide programs, publications and study groups, A.R.E. offers all those interested practical information and approaches for individual study and application to better understand and relate to themselves, to other people and to the universe. A.R.E. membership and outreach is concentrated in the United States with growing involvement throughout the world.

The headquarters at Virginia Beach, Virginia, include a library/conference center, administrative offices and publishing facilities, and are served by a beachfront motel. The library is one of the largest metaphysical, parapsychological libraries in the country. A.R.E. operates a bookstore, which also offers mail-order service and carries approximately 1,000 titles on nearly every subject related to spiritual growth, world religions, parapsychology and transpersonal psychology. A.R.E. serves its members through nationwide lecture programs, publications, a Braille library, a camp and an extensive Study Group Program.

The A.R.E. facilities, located at 67th Street and Atlantic Avenue, are open year-round. Visitors are always welcome and may write A.R.E., P.O. Box 595, Virginia Beach, VA 23451, for more information about the Association.